What Your Colleagues

"Nancy Akhavan has provided a much-needed, comprehensive approach to small-group literacy and language development for multilingual learners. She skillfully weaves research, theory, and application throughout the text while educating the reader about the unique needs of multilingual learners. This book values the assets multilingual students bring to the classroom and acknowledges the relationship between language and literacy development. *Small Group Reading With Multilingual Learners* provides an excellent resource to teachers, instructional coaches, and teacher educators seeking to enhance their understanding of small group literacy instruction for multilingual learners."

—Norma Carvajal Camacho
Assistant Superintendent of Educational Services,
Azusa Unified School District

"While there are many books on how to teach literacy to multilingual learners, few are as detailed and approachable as Nancy Akhavan's framework. As I read this book, I felt like I was being mentored by a highly skilled educator who patiently models how to turn principles of reading into practical actions for teachers of multilingual learners. I predict that this will be an invaluable resource for many who want to provide responsive, assets-based approaches to teaching MLs to read."

—Tan Huynh
English language development specialist, author, podcaster, blogger

"Nancy Akhavan began working with our district in 2020. She worked with . . . two pilot schools that were both willing and open to examining and changing their practices that would reduce the number of students qualifying for special education as well as realigning practices to concentrate on good first instruction. We have benefited from Nancy Akhavan's expertise and look forward to reducing overidentification of students as having a disability. *Small Group Reading With Multilingual Learners* can help districts, schools, and teachers to start this important work, too."

—Rebecca McHaney
Director of Special Services, Madera Unified School District

"In *Small Group Reading With Multilingual Learners*, Nancy Akhavan provides practical strategies for teaching foundational reading skills to multilingual learners at different stages of language development during small group reading instruction in just 20 minutes a day! An extensive menu of easy-to-implement strategies for each foundational reading skill makes this book especially practical for all elementary educators."

—Beth Skelton
Multilingual consultant

"Nancy Akhavan provides a fresh look at supporting multilingual learners. She provides educators with research-based, easy-to-understand educational practices. She provides implementation guides that help leaders of schools and classroom teachers systemize instruction. I've seen firsthand the shifts that can be made in classrooms when using Nancy Akhavan's recommendations and guidance. I highly recommend her book for any educator who wants to improve their practice."

—**Janet Samuelian**
Curriculum Administrator, Clovis Unified School District

Small Group Reading With Multilingual Learners

Differentiating Instruction in 20 Minutes a Day

Nancy Akhavan

FOR INFORMATION:

Corwin
A SAGE Company
2455 Teller Road
Thousand Oaks, California 91320
(800) 233-9936
www.corwin.com

SAGE Publications Ltd.
1 Oliver's Yard
55 City Road
London EC1Y 1SP
United Kingdom

SAGE Publications India Pvt. Ltd.
Unit No 323-333, Third Floor, F-Block
International Trade Tower Nehru Place
New Delhi 110 019

SAGE Publications Asia-Pacific Pte. Ltd.
18 Cross Street #10-10/11/12
China Square Central
Singapore 048423

President: Mike Soules
Vice President and
  Editorial Director: Monica Eckman
Executive Editor: Tori Mello Bachman
Content Development Editor: Sharon Wu
Editorial Assistant: Nancy Chung
Project Editor: Amy Schroller
Copy Editor: Karin Rathert
Typesetter: C&M Digitals (P) Ltd.
Proofreader: Lawrence W. Baker
Indexer: Sheila Hill
Cover Designer: Candice Harman
Marketing Manager: Margaret O'Connor

Printed in the United States of America

ISBN 9781071904145

This book is printed on acid-free paper.

23 24 25 26 27 10 9 8 7 6 5 4 3 2 1

Contents

CHAPTER NINE

For additional resources related to
Small Group Reading With Multilingual Learners,
visit the companion website at
resources.corwin.com/smallgroupreadingMLL.

About the Author

Nancy Akhavan, EdD, has spent more than 30 years as an educator and consultant. Her work focuses on student support through literacy instruction and intervention, English language development, leadership development, and organizational systems to increase student achievement. Currently, she is an associate professor in the Department of Educational Leadership at Fresno State. She is the founder of Nancy Akhavan Consulting, Inc. Dr. Akhavan has been a bilingual teacher, principal of three schools, and a district administrator of a large urban district for ELA, math, social studies, science, and world languages. She also served as Assistant Superintendent Secondary Division in a large urban school district. Dr. Akhavan is recognized for her expertise in teaching literacy practices. She has published 12 books that focus on instruction that increases student achievement and has worked with districts and county offices in multiple states and internationally to increase student achievement in reading, writing, and in content areas.

To all teachers who ensure students know the joy of multilingualism

An Abundance Mindset for Language Learning

iStock.com/martin-dm

Teaching multilingual students to read is one of the most reward-ing acts we do as teachers. I have been an educator for more than three decades, and I still get misty-eyed when I am sitting beside a child and "suddenly" her reading aloud of a text is fluent. After days or weeks or months of hard work, it all comes together—the young mind has enough understanding of English language words to decode, to understand meaning, and to read in the natural cadence of speech. There is no turning back! It's like watching a child finally ride a bicycle without wobbling.

I am writing this book so that all teachers can count on hav-ing these rewarding moments consistently, predictably, and

1

with all students. Many of the research-based strategies will be familiar to you, as they are effective for any child learning to read, but I have put them in a framework for teaching multilingual learners in a small-group setting. Let's begin!

WHAT'S NEW: TWO LANGUAGES AS AN ASSET

This resource is designed to help teachers do this work through a contemporary lens on teaching multilingual learners; the term *multilingual* signals an asset-based, abundant mindset about children who are adding English to their language abilities. Instead of the older term, "English language learners," the term "multilingual" communicates that we should all be so fortunate—and so wise—as to acquire more than one language in our lifetime.

Naturally, then, when we gather students at the reading table, we come with instruction that integrates English language development while supporting and leveraging students' home language, or heritage language.

iStock.com/FatCamera

Utilize Heritage Languages

Students' heritage languages provide support for them as they are acquiring English (Cummins, 2000; Genesee et al., 2005). Their heritage language helps them to communicate at greater levels of complexity as they learn about the world and connect culturally with their families and their traditions (Campos et al., 2011; Perez, 2004). So the very first thing we do to help a student acquiring English is to openly value their heritage language and cultural background. From planned curriculum to asking in-the-moment questions that invite children to share, there are many ways to do this work as teachers. When children see that we respect the languages they speak, it goes a long way toward making them feel central in the classroom community. Students' identity is tied to their heritage language, and so when educators openly or subconsciously convey that one language is more important than another language, the child feels diminished. All languages are important (Campos et al., 2011).

By extension, then, as teachers, we shift from an outdated mindset that we are *replacing* their heritage language with English. Instead, we embrace an additive approach. Our goal is to *add* English to their language repertoire.

> ## Terms of Note
>
> In this book, for simplicity, I often use the term *students* to mean multilingual learners who are acquiring English as an additional language. I also use *multilingual students* and *students whose first language is English* in order to make a distinction between these two groups of literacy learners.

Embrace Integrated English Language Development

The framework and strategies I describe in this book are considered *integrated* ELD strategies. Our instruction at the reading table is *integrated* ELD because we are providing support to students in language as well as in reading. By attending to both, we can be responsive to students' needs in each area simultaneously. Integrated ELD extends throughout the day; teachers incorporate strategies that help multilingual students understand the language and the content. It goes beyond the reading table.

Students acquiring English should receive both integrated and designated English language development (ELD). Research studies recommended that students receive a minimum of 30 minutes a day of designated ELD (Edelman et al., 2022). Edelman et al. found that students receiving 30 minutes of designated ELD at each grade level scored similarly to students who speak English as their heritage language by third grade as measured by English language knowledge assessments. ELD is specially designed instruction to help students increase their language acquisition in English (Wright, 2019).

Consider Current Research

The research on supporting English language development has exploded in the last decade. Following are some highlights:

- We know that multilingual learners who don't receive strong and systematic support may not designate and maintain their English learner status through high school.

- We know that developing learners' academic vocabulary is central to their success in reading nonfiction; without it, students struggle to gain content knowledge.

- Studies have shown that academic vocabulary acquisition supports continued language acquisition.

- High-challenge and high-support lessons are the most engaging for students.

- Teachers need assistance for developing these highly scaffolded lessons that integrate language, reading, and writing skills.

—Calderón and Slakk (2018); Calderón and Soto (2017); Echevarria and Vogt (2016); Gibbons (2015)

Throughout this book, I address what these five research highlights look like at the reading table; the last two about high-challenge and high-support lessons are ones I want you to consider a moment longer. Why? Because they speak to the need to differentiate instruction in small groups for multilingual students. This means that rather than simplifying the reading task, we need to increase the scaffolding (Gibbons, 2015). The bar has been raised, and yet, despite all we know from the last decade's research, most teachers feel wholly unprepared for the task. They haven't seen a clear model of what the instruction looks like. Teachers often ask me questions such as the following:

How do I form groups?

How much do I need to know the stages of English learner development?

Do I mix multilingual learners with students who are native English speakers?

What texts should we read together?

What about phonics?

Whew! This list of questions could go on and on, right? Take a deep breath. I've got your back. Following and in the chapters ahead, I share a new framework for supporting multilingual learners that reflects current research. It's also grounded in my expertise as a California-based professor who has specialized in working with students who have diverse and rich backgrounds and who are acquiring English as an additional language.

It puts together the research and work of Wayne Thomas and Virginia Collier, Jim Cummins, David and Yvonne Freeman, Diane August, and Kenji Hakuta with seminal teaching and learning theories of Vygotsky, P. David Pearson, and Gallagher, and important early reading and early literacy research by Birsch and Carreker (2018); Cunningham and Stanovich (1997); and Snow (2017). As such, it provides both the why and the how of what you do each day at the reading table.

Four Components for Teaching Multilingual Learners in Small Group Reading Lessons

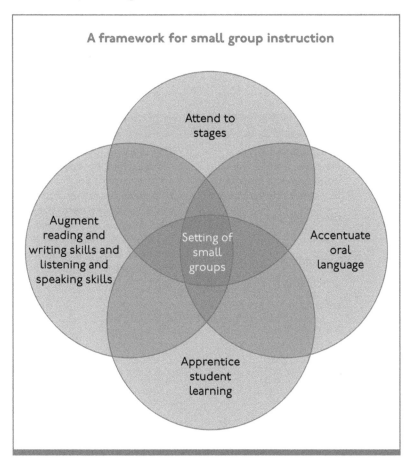

A framework for small group instruction

Attend to stages

Augment reading and writing skills and listening and speaking skills

Setting of small groups

Accentuate oral language

Apprentice student learning

THE FOUR COMPONENTS

Components	Research Support	Why It Matters
Attend to stages	Researchers have defined these stages of language development: entering beginning expanding bridging reaching	Knowing the stages of language acquisition will help you form groups, select texts, and plan lessons that teach into each student's current abilities and readiness for new learning.

Components	Research Support	Why It Matters
Apprentice student learning	Researchers Collins, Hawkins, and Carver contributed a helpful learning cycle as follows: modeling coaching scaffolding articulation reflection exploration	This is a valuable lesson model. Think of it as the architecture of your 20 minutes together. For multilingual learners, the model helps teachers use most of the small group lesson to coach, scaffold, and release students to work.

Components	Research Support	Why It Matters
Accentuate oral language	Researchers have added to our understanding of the critical importance of developing MLL's oral language. Students' ability to hear and speak develops before their ability to read and write; oral language provides opportunities for all learners to piece together letters and sounds and meaning. Oral language promotes fluency, a necessary skill for decoding and comprehension.	When multilingual learners come to our small group instruction, our role is to ensure that the language both in the books and as the language of conversation is understandable to every student. When students answer meaningful questions and talk with peers, it helps them understand ideas in texts and how those ideas relate to the world.

Components	Research Support	Why It Matters
Augment reading and writing skills and listening and speaking skills	A plethora of reading research supports instruction in the following skill areas: phonics oral language vocabulary word work comprehension writing to build reading comprehension oral language development	As researcher John Hattie writes, "Every student deserves a great teacher, not by chance, but by design" (Hattie, 2008). To teach multilingual learners, we have a responsibility to go about teaching language and reading systematically, focusing on the five reading skill areas with deep roots in research.

LEARNING ABOUT THE COMPONENTS IN THIS BOOK

iStock.com/SeventyFour

Readers grow with time and practice. When working with multilingual learners, you will be developing students' growth as a reader along with their growth in English language proficiency. Let's do a big-picture take on the components and where in this book you will learn more about them.

Attend to Stages

Multilingual students progress along a predictable continuum of stages of language acquisition. As the teacher, you use your awareness of each child's current stage to plan, implement, and adjust lessons. Each stage requires subtle shifts in your teaching at the small group table. *You will learn more about the stages in Chapter 1.*

Apprentice Student Learning

Students grow as readers when they have practice reading texts with you alongside them to help them. So in the most basic sense, small group instruction provides students with guided and independent practice reading texts; reading researchers agree, "eyes on print" is central to reading growth. Importantly, the quality of the teacher's "alongside them" coaching is the make-or-break factor in students' progress. It is for this reason that you use an apprenticeship model to scaffold independence. The framework spans from high teacher support (modeling) to lower teacher support (independent work). The six steps are the following: model, coach, scaffold, articulate, reflect, and explore.

Accentuate Oral Language

Talk is the foundation for thought and understanding—and human connection. I believe this whole heartedly, and I would go so far as to say that oral language development is the missing piece of the puzzle when it comes to teaching students to read—and especially those acquiring English. That's why I elevated it to be one of the four components. We know from research that MLLs acquire English for social reasons before academic ones (Cummins, 1981, 1996; Haynes, 2007), and so opportunities to talk and hear the language of peers are vital. We also know that choral reading and other oral language strategies help multilingual learners develop fluency.

Augment Reading and Writing Skills

This component is a big one! In Part II of this book, I devote entire chapters to Oral Language Development (Chapter 5), Phonics and Spelling (Chapter 6), Vocabulary (Chapter 7), Word Work (Chapter 8), and Comprehension (Chapter 9). To give you a taste of what's to come, here are some key details about each skill area.

Oral language instruction shows up in myriad ways at the reading table, from whisper reading, choral reading, book discussion, and talk between teacher and student during coaching and scaffolding.

Phonics and Spelling Instruction

The phonics and spelling instruction chapter will reflect the stages of the readers at the table; it's explicit, systematic, and tied directly to the text you are readings. Your main role is modeling the strategies they will use to *apply these foundational skills as they read* (Foorman & Conner, 2011). Phonics includes phonemic awareness, decoding and encoding, syllabication, and root words and affixes.

Vocabulary Instruction

This chapter discusses vocabulary instruction that is explicit, direct, and ongoing—even when students attain a high level of English language proficiency, you provide extra support before, during, and after reading. You expand students' vocabulary in terms of basic words, academic vocabulary, and content area vocabulary. And as is true with all these reading skills, you tie the work to the text you are reading, so it's meaningful. Expanding vocabulary helps all learners read increasingly complex texts and fortifies content knowledge—which, in turn, helps readers access challenging texts.

Word Work

Word work is an extension of phonics work combined with vocabulary development. It is teaching about how words are put together. Our goal is to help students figure out the word meanings for themselves. Word work at the early levels includes phonics, but at heart it's more sophisticated than decoding words. As students understand how English works and how word parts are put together in order to spell, word work morphs into vocabulary work. For example, when students work on compound words, root words, prefixes, and suffixes, they are compelled to attend to word meaning.

Comprehension

Students acquiring English may learn to decode the words before they understand everything that they are reading. However, reading is all about making meaning with text. It should be the focus from the beginning in reading instruction for all students. For multilingual learners, it's especially important to embed phonics work in the context of high-quality, engaging, meaningful texts and discussion so they can develop their oral language skills as well as their comprehension skills as they learn to read in English (Himmele & Himmele, 2009). Important comprehension strategies you will be teaching at the reading table include the following:

- Monitoring self for understanding

- Relating text to background knowledge

- Recounting or summarizing what was read

- Understanding text structure

- Synthesizing ideas and information from the text or from different texts

- Deductively thinking about text to identify cause and effect, compare and contrast, problem and solution, and sequencing

Writing to Build Reading

The chapter about writing honors that writing and reading are reciprocal processes. Young children solidify their understandings of recently learned phonics and reading skills when they apply them to writing. Writing tasks related to the text read in the small group lesson provides multilingual students with the chance to reread the text and use it as a scaffold for writing about it. Writing also consolidates their understanding of the text.

What's Unique to Multilingual Students

After this brief overview, let's pause to appreciate why learning to read is an especially steep climb for multilingual learners. Consider the following:

In the simplest terms, learning to be a fluent and accomplished reader involves the ability to decode text and use linguistic and background knowledge to understand what is read (Gough & Tunmer, 1986; Scarborough, 2001). But the task is different for multilingual learners. Helman et al. (2020, p. 8) describe it like this: "For [multilingual learners] this process is more complex . . . students are required to learn to read *what* the words mean at the same time they learn *how* to read them."

What All Learners Have in Common

If you are a K–2 teacher, this bird's eye view of the components will look familiar. That's because when we support multilingual learners, we are amplifying and augmenting what we always do in beginning-level reading instruction. If you are not a K–2 teacher, it's OK! Each chapter outlines the activities you can teach to build student reading skills. We want a tight connection between what students learn in phonics and what they encounter in the texts they are reading, so we use engaging, meaningful texts that provide sufficient challenges. We read and reread the texts together and individually to build fluency; we discuss the meaning to build and check comprehension and support oral language fluency; and we invite learners to apply their new understandings about phonics and words in writing. Emerging readers will be using their new knowledge about letters and sounds to write words and simple sentences. Fluent readers will use their knowledge of how words work to write about what they understand about what they read.

How This Book Is Organized

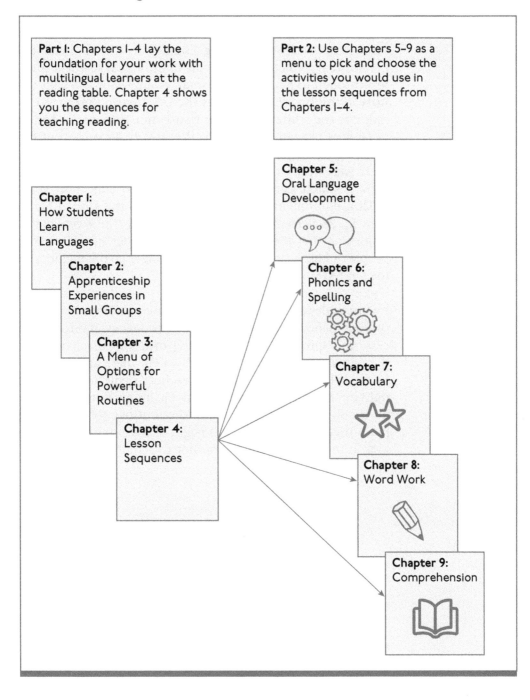

Part I: Chapters 1–4 lay the foundation for your work with multilingual learners at the reading table. Chapter 4 shows you the sequences for teaching reading.

Part 2: Use Chapters 5–9 as a menu to pick and choose the activities you would use in the lesson sequences from Chapters 1–4.

Chapter I: How Students Learn Languages

Chapter 2: Apprenticeship Experiences in Small Groups

Chapter 3: A Menu of Options for Powerful Routines

Chapter 4: Lesson Sequences

Chapter 5: Oral Language Development

Chapter 6: Phonics and Spelling

Chapter 7: Vocabulary

Chapter 8: Word Work

Chapter 9: Comprehension

Looking Ahead

I've given you a taste of the **why**, **what,** and the **how** of supporting students acquiring English. In the next chapter, I share the predictable stages all multilingual learners progress through to help you plan small group lessons. What's the **now** of this book? Estimates by the U.S. Census Bureau (2021) estimate the white population that is not Hispanic or Latino to be 60.4 percent. This means that nearly 40 percent of the U.S. population is of an ethnic or racial minority. In 2015, there were nearly five million English learners in U.S. schools (Pew Research Center, 2016). According to Education Week (2020), enrollment of English learners in the United States grew by 28 percent between 2000 and 2017. It is reasonable to assume that these figures are even higher now. By 2050, people of European ancestry will no longer be the majority in the United States.

I work with teachers every week of the year. I've seen them through pendulum swings in reading pedagogy, severe budget cuts, and spikes of teacher-bashing in the media. The stress the pandemic has caused teachers—well, there are no words. I have been made speechless by teachers' dedication to doing right by their students. With this book, it's my duty to do right by them, to provide easy-to-follow routines for supporting multilingual students. So let's begin at the beginning, with a look at the stages along the journey to acquire English.

Supporting Multilingual Learners

CHAPTER ONE

How Students Learn Languages

iStock.com/AJ_Watt

In this chapter, we focus on two facets of teaching multilingual students. First, we look at a continuum of language acquisition. Doing so helps us have a mental model of the stages in our minds as we teach and observe students during small-group instruction and beyond. Second, we look at the import of these stages through a cognitive and social-emotional lens and consider the implications for teaching. What are the stresses of acquiring English amidst twenty or more peers? What are these children's self-perceptions? What are the teaching methods that will align with research on building on students' strengths? I'm excited to share this information because it draws on recent studies from a range of disciplines, including neuroscience, linguistics, cognitive psychology, and popular psychology.

A CONTINUUM: DEVELOPMENT OF LANGUAGE LEARNERS

Students acquire language in a predictable flow. The flow is more of a continuum than a sequential "march" through discrete stages. Although your local or state assessments might label students as being at a particular "stage" of language acquisition at a given time, being able to envision it as a continuum is beneficial. Why? Because it reminds you that not every skill develops at the same pace and all children progress at different paces as well. In later chapters, I will detail how to leverage this fluidity to plan and deliver spot-on lessons.

Students move along the continuum of language acquisition from speaking their heritage language(s), to emerging as a multilingual student by adding one or more languages, and then becoming more and more fluent in both languages (Gottlieb, 2016; Wright, 2019). The stages along this continuum include the following: entering, emerging, developing, expanding, bridging, or reaching stages (Kohnert & Pham, 2010; Wright, 2019). The labels for the stages may vary slightly in different places; these are the labels used most by current researchers.

This continuum integrates the four domains of language: listening, speaking, reading, and writing. The four domains, also known as modes, do not develop at the same rate (Gibbons, 2015). Listening and reading are receptive modes, and speaking and writing are productive modes (in other words, students are producing language when they are speaking and writing). For instance, a student will understand more of what is said than what she can say, and a student will be able to say more than he can read or write, until they reach fluency in all four modes. Students are in different places on the continuum of development of each language mode at any given time. Now, let's look at the characteristics of each stage.

> This continuum integrates the four domains of language: listening, speaking, reading, and writing.

Entering

Students at the entering phase have minimal comprehension of what is being said. Students will not be speaking much or often. Their receptive modes are still developing. However, they can communicate through pointing, gestures, and drawing. They might demonstrate their comprehension abilities in the classroom, including the following: They can find or point

iStock.com/vejaa

to familiar objects, items, or people that are named orally for them. They can repeat simple phrases and words in unison with others. They can orally name objects they see—such as furniture in the classroom. They can also state personal likes and dislikes using pictures to help them.

Emerging

iStock.com/SDI Productions

Students at the emerging stage are beginning to use language— in particular, their listening and speaking abilities. Students at this level typically progress very quickly, learning to use English for immediate, interpersonal use and beginning to understand and use academic language that has been explained and contextualized. They may move through this stage in a few months to a year. They do have limited comprehension of what is said—however, they can speak in one- to two-word phrases, respond with familiar phrases, and use key words. They will form sentences using present-tense verbs. They can restate some language associated with texts and short stories. They can categorize and label. They can also connect oral language to print, state their preferences, describe uses of familiar objects, and participate in social interactions with peers.

Developing

iStock.com/FG Trade

Students developing language proficiency will speak in short sentences and begin to communicate more often socially. They will be able to follow sequential directions one step at a time, begin to write using sentence starters and drawings, and show relationships between ideas and objects. They can respond orally to show agreement or disagreement and state personal opinions. They will be able to communicate orally about content and give oral reports on content. They will be able to write statements about books read and connect ideas together. They will make frequent grammatical and pronunciation errors. Their use of verb tenses is expanding and they are beginning to learn irregular conjugations. They can identify details and key ideas in texts and make simple comparisons about text and story elements. They will be able to connect causal- or content-related relationships in texts together. For example, they will be able to identify cause and effect in texts that they read. They will know that different words are used to express similar ideas, and they will expand in their vocabularies both socially and with academic language.

Expanding

iStock.com/Courtney Hale

At the expanding stage, students' language proficiency is expanding beyond social language use, and they are beginning to use language for academic purposes more often. Students at this level need to be challenged to increase their English skills in more contexts and learn a greater variety of vocabulary and linguistic structures. They apply their language skills in more sophisticated ways and are able to produce statements about texts, convey their opinions, and explain information and ideas. You will notice students are now able to compare story elements and propose ideas to contribute to conversations. For example, they will be able to compare character actions to the development of the plot. They have good comprehension of social conversations, but they will not have complete comprehension of academic conversations. They will still make some errors in grammar and pronunciation. Academic conversations will need to be scaffolded. They will be able to use technical and specific vocabulary as well as identify multiple sources for ideas and information.

There are two categories of language students learn as they progress along the continuum of language acquisition: basic interpersonal communicative skills (BICS), or conversational language, and cognitive academic language proficiency (CALP), or academic language (Cummins, 1999). Multilinguals may be more proficient in one or the other at a given time. Consider both as you teach, support, and assess.

Bridging

iStock.com/MesquitaFMS

Students at this level continue to learn and apply a range of higher-level English language skills in some variety of contexts, including comprehension of and production of academic texts. They continue to need contextualized academic tasks. They will be able to back up opinions and write arguments. They will also be able to evaluate texts and books, including story and text elements and other literary elements and nonfiction text topics. They will be able to describe how factors relate in texts and lead to outcomes. They will be able to understand and use increasingly difficult academic vocabulary as they read texts that are comprehensible through the use of diagrams, pictures, and rich descriptions. They will be able to support claims with evidence from various sources and use claims and evidence to argue and persuade. They will make fewer grammatical and pronunciation errors but will still need academic language and tasks to be scaffolded.

Reaching

Students at this level continue to learn and apply a range of high-level English language skills in a wide variety of contexts, including comprehension and production of highly technical texts. They need far less contextualization of texts and ideas. They need minimal scaffolding of texts and information to be

iStock.com/ijeab

able to read, write, and discuss texts. They will use technical language connected to specific content areas and a variety of sentence lengths and sentences of varying complexity. They will be able to extend oral and written discourse in both fiction and nonfiction. Their oral and written communication in English is comparable to peers who are proficient in English (Krashen, 1988; Scarcella, 2003; WIDA, 2019; Wright, 2019).

Throughout this book, I will reference these stages in relation to specific activities that are especially apt for a stage.

ASSET LENS

Students acquire language when they are at ease, supported, and are invited to use language for purposeful classroom work. Remember to

- contextualize academic language by using pictures, diagrams, drawings, web-based videos, and so forth;

- discuss academic terms and content before launching into a lesson to frontload information, vocabulary, and ideas before launching into the lesson; and

- provide students time for reading authentic and engaging materials.

How Students Acquire English

Generally speaking, students acquire English in two ways. One way is by studying how English works and another way is by being immersed in understandable English used for authentic purposes. What I mean by *English that is understandable* is that the English being used to teach the lesson is comprehensible to students at their current stage of language acquisition. The student can comprehend what is being said or read. When language is comprehensible, students can understand and begin to talk; they basically begin to "pick up" how to express themselves (Krashen, 1988).

Students Embrace Social Communication First

Students will acquire English for social communication first before they acquire academic language. In other words, students will be able to communicate with you and with friends about daily matters before they can have an academic discussion about what they are reading (Krashen, 1982).

> Students will acquire English for social communication first before they acquire academic language.

The teaching take-away: Knowing that social communication comes before academic language is important, as throughout the day, we can motivate and encourage the peer talk that accelerates acquisition. However, at the reading table, our job is to focus on academics. Every child needs to learn the grade-level content and not be pandered to with "too-easy" texts. Instead, we accommodate multilingual learners (MLLs) by using interesting, relevant texts that have pictures, photos, and diagrams. We can also show additional pictures and videos that benefit all children learning to read. Pre-teaching vocabulary, as I'll detail in Chapter 7, is a highly effective tool. You can do this when introducing the book or at the point of the story when it's most appropriate.

Students Learn Language Best at the Edge of What They Know

Students acquire language when the language they are exposed to and working with is comprehensible. When something is comprehensible, it means that we can understand it. Krashen

(1982) studied language acquisition in multilingual learners and found that students best learn language when the language they are working with is just a little bit harder than what they can do on their own, without support.

I reference Stephen Krashen often in this book, as he is an American linguist and educational researcher whose work is central to teaching multilingual learners. His concept of using language that is "just a little bit harder" echoes Lev Vygotsky's learning theory, the zone of proximal development, or ZDP. The ZPD is the space between what a learner can do on their own, without assistance, and what they can do with assistance from adults or collaborating with peers (Billings & Walqui, n.d.). Every learner operates with the premise of *what I can do today with support, I can do tomorrow by myself.* So as teachers, we're always aiming to teach into a student's ZDP, ensuring what we are saying or asking isn't too easy or too hard but sufficiently challenging with our support. Krashen reminds us to use vocabulary that makes students work within a zone of optimum learning (Krashen, 1982).

The teaching take-away: Stretching students and using language with them that is just a little beyond their current level of comprehension ensures that we are expanding students' vocabulary and background knowledge. We want to avoid vocabulary that is so hard they shut down, but again, our job is to engage learners with new knowledge. For example, let's say you are reading a nonfiction text about photosynthesis. Before beginning the text, you could pull up a diagram or picture depicting photosynthesis on the web and add in arrows or point to the sun and then the plants and describe that this is how plants make food. You could highlight vocabulary in the text related to photosynthesis by opening the page to the book, pointing out the word, reading the sentence, and then discussing the word with the students to make sure they are grasping the idea or concept of the word. By showing pictures, locating vocabulary in context, and giving students time to think and talk through the concepts academic language represents, you will be making the vocabulary and the content comprehensible. With all you do, build on students' existing knowledge that they bring to the table—this knowledge is often referred to as "prior knowledge," and it's slightly different than the "content knowledge" associated with school.

iStock.com/Shutter2U

Students Progress Best With Highly Scaffolded Instruction

It makes intuitive sense that multilingual learners need high levels of support, especially at the first few stages of acquiring language. Even when they attain the reaching stage, you will continue to scaffold them at the reading table, assuring they continue to expand their vocabularies and other skills. It is for this reason that all the teaching ideas in this book fall under the umbrella of **sheltered instruction** (Echevarria & Graves, 2002), which is an approach that helps students who have some understanding of English develop academic skills and increase their English proficiency (Freeman & Freeman, 2014). Sheltered instruction focuses on the communication of ideas and helping students understand new learning even though they are still developing proficiency in English. This method includes the modification of grade-level content instruction. It highly scaffolds new learning so that students can understand the points that are being taught. Sheltered instruction depends heavily on using visuals to engage students while talking in English so that the students can understand what is being said.

In this book, I focus on teaching reading. This is not a book on teaching multilingual students English. I stress this point at the outset because designated ELD (English language development) instruction is strikingly different than teaching reading to multilingual students alongside students whose first language is English.

ASSET LENS

Speaking more slowly is a powerful strategy! Check to make sure you aren't talking too fast by inviting another teacher to watch a lesson or by videoing a lesson.

Students Learn Language When They Belong

Another important theory of Krashen (1982) is the idea that students acquire language when they are comfortable and supported. Called the *affective filter,* the premise of the theory is that when a student is emotionally distraught or socio-emotionally not supported in the classroom and in their learning environments, it will be difficult to acquire language. The fear of making mistakes in front of peers impedes their ability to learn. It can be hard for students to take risks when speaking or writing in English.

By contrast, in low-anxiety learning settings, student motivation, esteem, and self-confidence remain high, making it more likely that students will be able to focus on the lesson and the language being used in the lesson (Peregoy & Boyle, 2016). Safety and security come first for students, and they need to feel safe and secure at the reading table as well. Admonishment or "holding students responsible" for some point in learning in a negative way will not help students acquire English.

The teaching take-away: In order to keep negative emotions low and positive emotions high, do an audit of your routines at the small group reading table. Following are some fairly simple solutions that ease students' anxiety and allow you to stay true to instructional goals.

Common triggers for negative emotions	Solutions to Ease Students' Anxiety
Composition of reading group	Have flexible grouping.
	Sometimes group students with other students who are language learners so that the focus can be on discussing and using language in ways that are comfortable for the multilingual learners.
	Always group students with buddies who make them feel comfortable or who can help them.
	Sometimes group students by reading acquisition level in order to support the reading level or reading strategy being worked with.
Pressure to speak	When students are beginning to learn English, keep pressure low.
	As students acquire language, encourage them to speak, but never demand that they speak. If they don't want to speak, find other ways that they can express themselves, perhaps whisper talking only with you or with a friend or writing their thinking down.
Pressure to read aloud	Focus on having them reading aloud only to themselves (when others are simultaneously reading aloud so the students realize no one will be listening to them), and/or invite them to read aloud to you or whisper read (perhaps using a whisper phone), or do not have them read aloud at all if they are becoming fairly fluent readers and need to work on pronunciation and vocabulary "in their head" before saying it out loud.
Errors	Be accepting of errors and encourage students to talk. They don't need to say things perfectly. Instead of correcting orally, model by restating what the student said, but say it the correct way. In writing one-on-one, pick one or two points and teach the correct way of writing the word or sentence, but don't pick on everything. Be positive about errors; the more students talk and write, the more their errors will naturally decrease!
Composition of the group at the table	Supportive groups are best. It doesn't matter if they are homogenous or heterogenous; what matters is you develop a classroom culture of respect of all students, not only students learning English.
Presentation of language	Focus on comprehension + just a little bit more. Use realia—pictures, diagrams, videos, and so forth, ensure language is understandable. Using hands-on manipulatives, whiteboards, virtual whiteboards, flashcards, sentence strips, writing journals, laptops (for multimedia), magnetic letters, magnetic word tiles, and other tactile tools supports students as they learn language.

Looking Ahead

In this chapter, I've explored what it means to "attend to stages" of language development. Probably the most important take-away is to recognize that teaching multilingual students at the reading table doesn't require an entirely new bag of tricks. In the next chapter, we move onto the second component, **apprenticeship learning**. Here is where you get to lean on a research-based teaching and learning model for small group work.

CHAPTER TWO

Apprenticeship Experiences in Small Groups

iStock.com/FatCamera

We turn now to your specific actions during small group work. The information in this chapter provides you with the structure you will lean on as you learn specific routines in later chapters.

The steps of teaching and learning are adapted from the work of Collins, Hawkins, and Carver. These three researchers described the need for apprenticeship-like experiences in the classroom (Collins et al., 1991).

An apprentice works closely with a more skilled other to learn a trade; it's as old as human civilization, of course! Collins et al. focused on the idea of *cognitive apprenticeship*, wherein the learner closely observes and then emulates the ways of thinking of the more skilled teacher. They made the point that in modern society, with greater numbers of students, schooling has made the apprenticeship model difficult, as it requires a very small teacher-to-learner ratio. But guess what? In small-group instruction, the model can thrive.

GIVING MULTILINGUAL STUDENTS THE PRACTICE THEY NEED

The apprenticeship model is especially beneficial for multilingual learners because it helps teachers be mindful that students are doing the work, not you. The model helps you teach within their zone of proximal development. As students stretch themselves to read more difficult and demanding texts and learn vocabulary along the way, they require you to step back. Do less, so they can do more. Doing less means focusing on their exact needs through scaffolding and coaching (Akhavan & Walsh, 2020). Doing less means precision and responsive scaffolding, as opposed to heavy I-do modeling that leads to rote learning. Beginning on page 42, I'll go into more detail about how to apply the gradual release of responsibility model (Pearson & Gallagher, 1983) almost as an overlay to the apprenticeship model.

A Recursive Model

Apprenticing is not a linear model. You can start in one place in the model and move to another (see following graphic). For instance, a student might say that she is having a problem reading a word in a book and tell you she doesn't know how to sound it out (*articulation*); you could suggest a tactic the student take in being able to figure out the word, perhaps looking at the root and then figuring out the meaning (*scaffolding*). You could model how to do this for the student based on the roots that you have been studying in class (*modeling*).

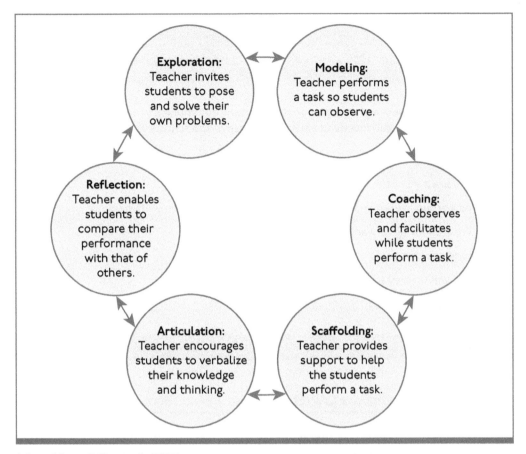

Adapted from Collins et al. (1991).

While it doesn't matter where you start in the process of cognitive apprenticeship, what is important to note is that when you model, coach, and scaffold, you encourage students to work out their reading trouble and then articulate what they are doing, reflect on what they tried, and then extend the learning to new texts that they are working to read. By taking these steps, you can empower students as readers and increase the effectiveness of your work at the reading table.

ASSET LENS

Share with students a philosophy of your learning community. In and beyond the reading table, all students need a palpable sense of the following:

- You belong here.

- You are part of the community.

- As a group, we won't accept behavior that gets our learning off-track.

- We are moving forward.

- I will support you.

- You will understand.

—Akhavan (2007)

Find a Swift Tempo

Effective literacy instruction has a lively, engaging pace. When working with multilingual students, pacing is important. In my work with teachers, the two most common challenges they have are talking and moving through a lesson too quickly and doing too much of the work for the student. The speed you want to adopt at the reading table isn't so fast-paced that it leaves students behind in the dust, but it certainly shouldn't drag either. Instruction needs to target what they need to know and move at a pace that is motivating and engaging and supports all learners so they have the chance to understand (Perry et al., 2006).

APPRENTICING IN ACTION

iStock.com/Weedezign

Let's look at classroom examples of each teacher and learner role in action. With only twenty minutes a day for this work with students, you'll find the need to watch the clock until you feel comfortable integrating the phases of instruction. The biggest challenge might be watching your time and keeping on track. Make sure you are not eating up too many precious minutes with modeling.

Modeling at the Reading Table

What we model at the reading table depends on our learning target and our objective. We might be focused on increasing students' foundational skills in reading, and our objective could be teaching students to break their reading text into parts (chunk it), read (read it), and then stop and think about what they read saying or writing their thoughts out (say it). If I were working on this reading strategy, I would model how I planned to chunk the text I was reading, then read the section and stop where I had planned to stop, and then retell what the text said. Then I would say, "Did you notice what I just did? I decided on a stopping point in the text; I read until the place I chose to stop; and then I thought about what I read and I said out loud what the text said." It is important in modeling to explicitly point out what it is that we are modeling before

> What we model at the reading table depends on our learning target and our objective.

we model it and restate what we did right after we model it (chunk it, read it, say it).

Strategy: Chunk it, read it, say it

- Chunk it: Students predetermine what amount of text they will read.

- Read it: Students read the text, stopping at the predetermined point.

- Say it: Students reflect on what they read, discuss it with an elbow partner or with the teacher, or write their thoughts in a notebook.

We can model how to

- Sound out words

- Read out loud in front of students

- Read silently for a few seconds

- Think while speaking out loud about what we read

- Write about what we read

- Write letters, words, and sentences

- Use graphic organizers

- Think out loud while using graphic organizers

Coaching at the Reading Table

We coach readers at the reading table. When students are with us at the reading table, they are mostly reading on their own. We may be reading to them, and we may be reading with them, but we need to keep these two activities short. We need to focus on students reading on their own with us there to coach and support them as they read. We are supporting them as they figure out the words for themselves and work on comprehension.

> **When students are with us at the reading table, they are mostly reading on their own.**

Younger readers read out loud (they can whisper read so it's not too loud), and more experienced readers most likely will read to themselves. While they are reading, we support them so that they can be successful with attacking words and also maintain comprehension. The students are doing the work, not us. The students own the cognitive lift. When their brains are doing the work, they will be more engaged. If we do the reading work (we answer our own questions, we read aloud all the time and don't design opportunity for student independent reading), too often students will likely become disengaged and feel like they are not progressing (Helman, 2016a, Helman 2016b). Because they are reading text that stretches them, we are there to help them.

Often when students are reading on their own, I ask them to read for me a few lines so that I can check their accuracy and fluency. As I lean in and listen to students read, I coach actions they can take when they come to words they don't know (I want them to attack the word, not skip it). I would remind students of decoding and word work strategies that we have worked on together as a group in the past as they read to me so that I can reinforce their actions and encourage them to keep working on their own.

We can coach to support independent reading for emerging readers by

- Reminding them to look at the beginning of the word and begin to sound out the word

- Reminding them to look all the way through the word

- Reminding them to chunk the word into syllables and sound out the syllables

- Reminding them to look for sounds they know in the word like *-er* or *-ing*

We can coach to support independent readers/fluent readers by

- Focusing students on fluent reading, phrasing, and intonation

- Modeling for and guiding students to read fluidly and with expression

- Reminding students to stop and think about what they have read, and if they don't know, then reread

- Helping students figure out the meaning of unknown words by rereading

- Guiding students to visualize what they are reading so they can see a "movie in their minds"

- Asking them to stop reading and paraphrase what they have read

- Guiding them to make connections while reading to their life experiences, something they know or have learned, or something that they have seen and heard before

ASSET LENS

The clearer we are in our teaching, the clearer students are in what is expected of them. Our multilingual learners need to know that we have their backs—that we are consistently attending to these three things, for their benefit:

1. Directing their use of reading strategies

2. Guiding their use of vocabulary—working over time to make sure they don't get lost, that they understand basic vocabulary, that they understand the vocabulary in the books in front of them, and that they understand the academic and content vocabulary that relates to the text

3. Scaffolding them toward independence, using tools, talk, and text to make sure they are taking over the work of fluent engaged reading

Scaffolding at the Reading Table

We scaffold for multilingual students by using some of the same supports as we did when students were emergent and early readers, but as they expand their language proficiency, we scaffold by having them rely on tools that help them comprehend. The tools themselves are scaffolds—such as dialogue journals, response journals, sticky notes, 3-2-1-exit cards, personal word dictionaries, and personal word rings. But notice that the work they do falls into the reflection zone of the apprenticeship model. This is a good example of how the model is recursive and there are blurred lines between the six phases.

We can scaffold for readers by

- Offering/using a concrete tool, such as a graphic organizer, sound boxes, or a clothespin for spacing while writing.

Tactile scaffolds are there to make the language we use and the content more comprehensible.

- Offering a supportive process, such as referring to a high frequency word wall, or a succinct strategy, such as Read it, chunk it, write it.

We scaffold when

- Teaching a reading skill or strategy
- Students read on their own
- Students discuss their comprehension of what they have read
- Students write about their reading
- Students write, working with spelling and word patterns

We can scaffold new to English or emergent readers by

- Working with letters, sounds, and sight words (see Chapter 6). Using magnetic letters, letter cards, sound cards, and realia so they are able to touch, label, or handle everyday objects
- Showing pictures, using videos on a device to teach vocabulary, and writing on whiteboards to practice letters and words

We can scaffold students growing in proficiency in English and/or who are early readers by

- Using the scaffolds stated previously
- Providing sentence strips and sentence frames; helping students be able to form sentences
- Using word cards to have students manipulate words and sentences in pocket charts
- Using sentence-building cards for students to manipulate sentence creation
- Creating word banks with pictures to develop students' vocabularies
- Labeling known items
- Highlighting and posting words associated with everyday objects and information students are learning about

Articulation at the Reading Table

Students will be talking about what they are reading from the first moment they pick up a book. **We develop articulation by having students**

- Discuss their books in single words and short phrases (at first).

- Talk about their thinking about what they are reading with more depth or what they are working on with you related to reading (once they are ready). See more about oral language development in Chapter 6.

- Discuss their reading in short statements once they are at the developing stage.

As they grow in language acquisition, their sentences will be longer and more content specific based on their reading. What they will be able to discuss and how they talk about it will increase as they grow. For example, students at the developing stage may not yet talk in full sentences but rather talk in longer phrases. As they grow and develop their English proficiency, they will be able to discuss more and at more length. See the following general guidelines about what is reasonable to expect in student discussions based on their language acquisition level. This recaps information in Chapter 1, but it's helpful to see it again in the context of articulation.

Entering	Students can point, gesture, draw, act out.
Emerging	Students can speak in one- to two-word phrases, respond with familiar phrases, and use key words. They will form sentences using present-tense verbs.
Developing	Students can speak in short sentences and begin to communicate more often socially.
Expanding	Students begin to use language for academic purposes more often. They will be able to produce statements about texts, convey their opinions, and explain information and ideas.
Bridging	Students will be able to back up opinions and write arguments and evaluate texts and books, including story and text elements and other literary elements and nonfiction text topics. They will be able to understand and use increasingly difficult academic vocabulary. They will be able to support claims with evidence from various sources and use claims and evidence to argue and persuade.
Reaching	Students will use technical language connected to specific content areas and use a variety of sentence lengths and sentences of varying complexity.

In Chapter 6, you will learn more about discussion and oral language and what to expect based on students' language acquisition level.

Reflection at the Reading Table

When students reflect on their reading, they can check their own progress and engage in goal setting. This is a good practice for students, as when they are aware of their own learning, they can celebrate what they have accomplished and set their sights on learning new words to expand their vocabularies.

Reflection is most effective when

- Paired with self-regulation and feedback from the teacher

- It involves helping the student with greater skill in self-regulation use strategies that have been taught (Hattie, 2008). For example, "You already know a lot of cognates. Apply what you know about cognates to the words in this text." Or "You already know the features in an opinion piece, see if you can identify the author's point."

- Feedback from the teacher is coupled with student self-reflection. (This helps students apply what they know and see a purpose in applying new learning to their reading and writing.)

Exploration at the Reading Table

Students at the **bridging** and **extending** levels of language proficiency will be ready to pose and solve their own problems.

We support exploration by having students

- Work with you at the reading table on content-area reading where they need extra support.

- Work on knowledge development when reading content area texts through vocabulary discussions. (Knowledge building is the sixth pillar of reading [Hiebert, 2019].)

- Expand their ability to comprehend multiple types of texts by varying genres.

Often English learners need additional help with the reading they encounter during science and social studies, and you can bring these texts to the reading table to help them with the vocabulary and understand the concepts the words represent.

Now that you have the six apprenticeship steps in mind, I want you to pause to notice how these steps are really an expansion of the gradual release of responsibility model (Pearson & Gallagher, 1983). As I pointed out in the introduction, research on teaching multilingual learners has all pointed to one conclusion: These learners need to work with grade-level content and have the benefit of a teacher who knows how to harness the power of differentiated instruction. High-challenge, high-scaffold lessons are paced and orchestrated so students spend time working in their ZDP, in the you-do phase.

FAVORING THE "YOU-DO" PHASE

Most of our students need more time talking, working, and trying during small-group instruction—and throughout the day. Teachers tend to model and talk too much. For multilingual learners, it's even more urgent that we refrain from well-intentioned but hyper-helping! We meet with small groups for twenty to twenty-five minutes. We might teach directly the "I do" for five minutes and spend five to seven minutes with the "we do." But the most minutes—seven to ten minutes—are devoted to the "you do." As shown in the following graphics, you will take your cues on I do, we do, and you do based on the stages of your multilingual learners. And remember, it's not a lockstep, linear process; you can swing back to modeling or collaborative work whenever you sense the need for reteaching and greater support.

I Do: Direct Instruction Phase

The I-do phase is short so that multilinguals have ample time to read and practice. Try to keep it to three minutes; no more than five. It's clear and direct, offering a single teaching point for a single purpose (figuring out words, developing fluency, inferring, for example). You model a single strategy so learners can focus and apply more easily. Day by day, model by model, you teach a variety of skills.

> We meet with small groups for twenty to twenty-five minutes. We might teach directly the "I do" for five minutes and spend five to seven minutes with the "we do." But the most minutes—seven to ten minutes—are devoted to the "you do."

Give students time to do the word with you at the table with you supporting.

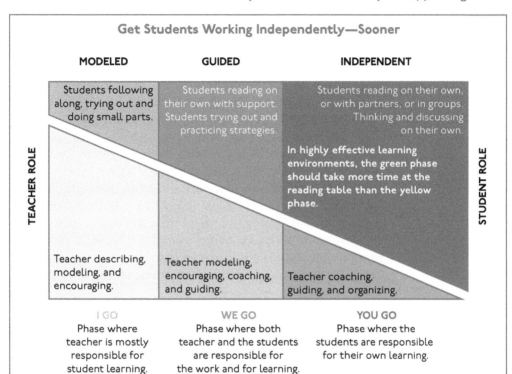

Reprinted with permission of Benchmark Education from the book *At the Reading Table, Striving Readers: Achieving Equity by Scaffolding Strengths.*

We Do: Supportive Phase

In the we-do phase, we coach as students apply the strategy to their reading. It's five to seven minutes; as we see students in group ready to read independently, we can signal to them to go for it and have them slide into the you-do phase. This frees us up to do work together with the students who we see struggling a bit to do tasks that are beyond their language proficiency level. To avoid them getting frustrated and shutting down, we scaffold. We do this by sharing an additional strategy or having on hand from the get-go manipulatives, pictures, diagrams, and videos to build understanding of the language expectations. To accomplish this, we can use whiteboards, virtual whiteboards, flashcards, sentence strips, writing journals, laptops (for multimedia), picture books, predictable texts, magnetic letters, magnetic word tiles, nonfiction text filled with text features, and real objects to help us demonstrate language meaning.

You Do: Independent Phase

Whether students are emerging as multilingual learners, expanding in their language abilities, or bridging to higher levels of fluency, we will provide opportunities for students to be in the independent phase of the GRR. We want them to be in the independent phase more quickly because the more students read (on their own with us coaching and supporting), the more time they will have to read. Also, we don't have a lot of time at the reading table, and we need to be mindful of reading volume. The more students practice their reading with us there to support and guide through effective feedback, the greater their learning will be (Hattie, 2008). The better they will be able to read. During the you-do phase, you are focused on feedback. When you give feedback to students based exactly on what you see them doing while they are reading independently, you can guide them to us the skills and strategies they know.

Looking Ahead

In this chapter, I used the apprenticeship model to help you think about your role at the reading table as model and coach. In the next chapter, I share *all* the routines you can select from for your lessons. They span listening, speaking, reading, and writing. I call it a *menu of options*, and every item on it supports both language acquisition and reading development.

CHAPTER THREE

A Menu of Options for Powerful Routines

One of the most common questions teachers often ask me about teaching multilingual students is, *What are the best routines to use with small group instruction?* I've discovered that the most effective answer—and a crowd favorite—is to give teachers a big menu of options first. And then later, go into greater specifics of how to put the options into lesson sequences. So let's get started. And by menu, I mean classic diner menu! The one that weighs three pounds, is eight pages long, and has an entire page devoted to omelets. Jest aside, teachers I work with find it helpful to have *all* the options for small group routines in one place. The routines, whether it's shared reading or close reading, bring the specific reading skills instruction alive. In Part II of this book, I provide a lot of practical ideas for teaching the specific reading skills—oral language, phonemic awareness, phonics, spelling, vocabulary, word work, comprehension, and writing—to build reading. As we will explore beginning on the next page, we develop readers by developing writers, so you will find lots of attention to both these reciprocal processes.

Routines That Develop Readers and Writers

In the next section, I show you how to adapt research-based literacy routines for multilingual learners. I will cover reading routines and then writing routines.

> At the reading table, you will be tethering these reading and writing routines together into a dynamic lesson sequence.

At the reading table, you will be tethering these reading and writing routines together into a dynamic lesson sequence (see Chapter 4). Each day and across the week, these sequences ensure students get varied experiences. The routines involve the four domains of language: listening, speaking, reading, and writing. They involve purposeful attention to expanding vocabulary and scaffolds for comprehending the texts we read so that we lift up multilingual learners, providing them with a holistic experience of reading that is meaningful and motivating.

Choral Reading

Beyond the reading table, choral reading can be done as a whole class, in pairs, and for independent practice.

The benefits: Multilingual learners at **emerging** and **developing** levels of English language acquisition begin with choral reading, before they go on to read on their own. Through choral reading, we can model fluency, including intonation and prosody. Choral reading also allows students to hear you pronounce words that might still be challenging for them. As we read, we model how reading sounds when read fluently. The teacher's reading is expressive, a reflection of *understanding* the text, so students get opportunities to in a sense hear what comprehension sounds like.

How to do it: In choral reading, we read aloud and students, with a copy of the book in front of them, read along with us. (You can do choral reading with big books or chart poems, too.) You can use a Smart board to project the text so students can read without having the text right on their desks. To start choral reading, ensure that you are telling students where you will start reading and give a signal to start everyone reading together. Throughout, while you are reading aloud, your mind is listening—noticing each student and what they may need continued support with.

Text selection tips: For **emergent** readers, patterned texts or predictable texts work well. Poems, songs, and book excerpts are great throughout all levels of proficiency. Remember to use choral reading to support students with text that might be too hard to read on their own. Once they can handle the text on their own, give them opportunities to read independently.

Practice tips: Provide students with individual copies of the texts from the lesson or select additional texts for practice with peers and at home. During the day or at home, students can choral read with a peer, and each can even take a different part of a text (for example, using a poem of two voices or a short script). Older readers enjoy choral reading song lyrics. When assigning partnerships for this practice, it can be beneficial to put two students of varying abilities together and give each student a different section of a poem or passage to read.

Shared Reading

Beyond the reading table, shared reading can be done as a whole class and in small groups.

The benefits: Shared reading is wonderful for students who are at the **entering** and **emerging** levels of language acquisition and sometimes for students at the **developing** level. Why? It feels less daunting for them than choral reading or independent reading because the responsibility is shared. Students new to English tend to go through a phase called "the silent period," which is when they are taking language in, making connections between what they are hearing and what the words mean (Bao, 2014). So a choral read, where you rapidly move through the text and students are expected to read with you, is intimidating.

How to do it: In shared reading, students have a copy of the book or text and follow along with you as you read aloud. Point to the words as you read, and slow down your pace so students learning English can track with you. They won't be able to read with you yet, but they listen as you model; you can pause and take the time to work through vocabulary in the text and also point out sight words or words you have been practicing decoding together. You can also reinforce phonemic awareness during shared reading (Ukrainetz et al., 2000). You can begin the shared reading by talking about the book—what the book was about and the words in the book—to develop oral language skills. This is very short—you might take three to four minutes to introduce the book and review important vocabulary.

You can continue discussing what you are seeing and reading about in the book as you go along. Make sure and stop along the way and discuss new terms, new ideas, or words and information that may be unfamiliar for students. It is more effective to teach the new vocabulary as you go along so that the words are introduced within the context of the text. When you are discussing words while reading, take enough time to ensure students are comprehending the word meaning. This might take time. You don't have to read the entire text during one lesson; you can revisit the book or text again on another day.

Text selection tips: For students who are **emergent** readers, big books and texts at appropriate level of complexity work well. For students who are more **fluent** readers, continue to use text at the appropriate level of complexity, which can include books, text from your district's adopted matierials, or texts from an online source. Avoid using picture books, as the language may be too sophisticated (picture books work well as read alouds). Students often gravitate to nonfiction texts on topics they are interested in.

Practice tips: When students are ready to work together in pairs or small groups, they can practice shared reading together. The students can read together and then stop and talk about what they are seeing and noticing in the book. It is best to have students do a shared reading together in a book or text that you have previously introduced so that multilingual learners will have the modeling and discussion of the book's new ideas, vocabulary, and information fresh in their minds.

Focusing on Concepts of Print During Shared Reading

During shared reading, you can focus on teaching concepts of print. Through your book discussion, you can stop and point out features of text that students need to learn.

When working with younger students who have not yet developed knowledge about books, you can model and coach the following:

- Relationship between print and spoken words

- Distinction between sentences, words, and letters

- Spacing between words

- Mechanics, like punctuation, that provide meaning and understanding

- Book orientation and direction of print

- Parts of a book (Clay, 1993)

If you are working with older students who already know how to read in their heritage language, you may not need to teach concepts about print, as the students will most likely have developed these skills earlier. That said, I suggest you do some research about concepts of print in the students' heritage language to determine which, if any, concepts of print need to be taught. If they read in a language where the text is written right to left, like Farsi, you will need to point out that English moves left to right and discuss the front of the book and where sentences begin. However, this may only take one lesson, as students who are literate understand the concept of how the print works but may just need some guidance. It is important to remember that students' literacy in their heritage language can vary greatly depending on their prior schooling experiences. Some may be able to speak and comprehend their heritage language but may not have the skills to read and write.

Text selection tips: Use simple text that provide opportunities to showcase the concepts. Big books, story books, text at appropriate levels of complexity, decodables, and web-based text work well.

Practice tips: Hand out books or text to students and review the concepts with them that you have taught. You can ask students to identify these concepts. Students can point to show you the answers to your questions. Students can also practice independently when writing about their reading. They can practice adding spaces between words, writing in the direction you have taught, and work to make their handwriting legible.

Big Books

Multilingual learners benefit from visual support, and so big books are a favorite tool of mine. As the name implies, they are giant versions of fiction and nonfiction, often 13 X 19 inches or larger. Students at the reading table can easily see the words and illustrations. You can find them on Amazon or other educational websites when you search for "big books for shared reading." They are part of many reading programs as well.

Close Reading

Close reading is a type of shared reading. Close reading means reading a short text intentionally with a specific purpose in mind with each read. Close reading helps students notice text features and develop deeper understanding of texts. Beyond the reading table, you can do this routine as a whole class, but it doesn't lend itself to independent practice. In other words, we hope students apply the principles as they read on their own, of course, but we don't want students to do all six steps on their own.

The benefits: Multilingual learners at the **expanding** level may still need shared reading; however, students at the **bridging** and **reaching** levels need to move to close reading. In close reading, you provide support for students with language, focusing on concept and vocabulary while reading complex texts. You facilitate the thinking process for students, but you don't do the thinking for them. This is especially important for multilingual learners because students discuss, providing their own thoughts and ideas. There is no one right way to process text during a shared reading. The *one right thing to do* is to only facilitate and not "do the doing" for the students by doing the thinking for them (Akhavan, 2019).

How to do it: When students are involved in close reading, they are deeply examining a text, considering the author's thinking and point of view and gathering evidence from the text to reinforce their claims about the meaning and purpose of the text. There is a distinct and specific purpose for each read of the text. Some of the student abilities include

- Cite textual evidence

- Determine central ideas of text

- Trace and evaluate the argument and specific claims in a text

- Ask and answer questions and refer explicitly to text as a basis for answers

- Quote accurately from a text when explaining what the text says explicitly

Steps to a close reading involve reading the passage more than once, building understanding of the text and making meaning with each reading and each discussion of the text.

1. Students read through the text one time. They "graze."

2. Go through the text as a group and paraphrase sentences. They can annotate as they work.

3. Students read the text again on their own with you facilitating, focusing closely on what the text says. Annotate as appropriate.

4. Discuss as a group what the text says.

5. Students read the text a third time, focusing on meaning. They can annotate as they read.

6. Discuss deep meaning together.

Book selection tips: Choose texts that are shorter in length, about one or two pages, or use an excerpt of text. Any text type works well, but texts that are rich in content and ideas work best so there are lots of interesting points for student to work with.

Practice tips: Once students know the routine of close reading, invite them to close read a book section, short text, or text excerpt before meeting with the group. Students can work through Steps 1 through 3 and Step 4 on their own and then, using their notes, you can facilitate a conversation about the text. By having students work independently first, you can involve students in rich discussions about texts that they have had time to dig into independently.

Independent Reading

Students will be reading with you at the table and reading on their own when they are working independently. When students are reading with you at the reading table, you are there to facilitate their reading and thinking. Students who normally read silently don't need to read aloud at the reading table. We want to avoid round robin reading because it doesn't engage all students—it is hopeful to think that students are processing text while another student is reading aloud. Reading at the table should be about students working through text, processing the text for themselves; that said, silent reading is best, even in front of you. You can always lean in and ask a student to read to you to check fluency. Another option is pair reading. Students can pair together and read to each other at the reading table, and then you can reconvene the group for discussion.

After students work with you at the reading table, they need to read away from you with independent, sustained reading. Twenty to thirty minutes of reading independently increases students' reading ability, increases their fluency as they work through text, and increases their comprehension as they practice the skills and strategies you have taught at the reading table (Fisher et al., 2019). The more students read, the better reader they will become (Cipielewski & Stanovich, 1992). The more students read each day, the more words they will read per year. Anderson et al. (1988) conducted seminal research on sustained reading that has been validated many times over in recent years (Fisher et al., 2019). In these studies, Anderson et al. found a correlation between the volume of reading a student did per year and their performance on standardized tests given in the spring. Students who read more scored at higher percentile levels. Students who read approximately twenty minutes per day scored in the ninetieth percentile on standardized tests, and students who read approximately five minutes per day scored in the fiftieth percentile (Cipielewski & Stanovich, 1992; Krashen & Mason, 2017; Robb, 2000; Steitz et al., 2016; Wang & Gutherie, 2004). Building on reading that you launch at the reading table and having students continue on their own are important.

> Twenty to thirty minutes of reading independently increases students reading ability.

The benefits: You will encourage students to read independently all at once at the reading table. Use your minutes in small group wisely. Don't make students listen to each other read; they need to spend the maximum time reading on their own. Encourage independent reading, and you can check in with each student to check their decoding skills and comprehension. If independent reading is too difficult because the students have not yet acquired enough English to be successful, incorporate choral or partner reading (Montero & Kuhn, 2016). Don't take time with students reading one at a time, as you want all the students' thinking focused on how they will apply their skills to read the words for themselves.

How to do it: Coaching during independent reading might look different for each student. You would encourage your students to use their automatic word recognition skills and phonetic analysis skills with real text (Walpole & McKenna, 2007). After introducing the text, invite students to begin independent reading. **Emergent** and **early** readers will most likely be reading aloud, so encourage them to whisper read. Students who are more fluent readers can read silently. If you are using a U-shaped table, you can lean in and listen to different students read aloud and provide tips on how to read the words or encourage them to think about what they have read. If students seem to be reading along well, talk with them for a few seconds, perhaps up to a minute or more, to check on their level of comprehension. For students who are having trouble saying the words or reading fluently, spend more time reminding them how to sound out words.

When students are reading independently, you want to encourage them to use the phonics strategies that you have been teaching to read the words (or decode). You can also focus on fluency and phrasing. For comprehension, check in with students on what they are understanding about what they have read. Remind them of the comprehension strategies you have been teaching the group. You can coach them to use these strategies. Direct students' attention to sound and spelling patterns first and then use syntactic clues to see if their efforts to decode were correct (Walpole & McKenna, 2007). When students need support in figuring out words, you might say things like the following:

- "Use your sounds; what is the first sound in the word?"

- "What do you know about that sound/word? What are you going to do?"

- "What is the next sound in the word?"

- "Can you blend the sounds together? What word did you read?"

- "Does that word make sense in the sentence?"

- "Use what you know about sight words to read that word."

- "What do you know about that sound/spelling pattern?"

Text selection tips: Use texts on topics that students are interested in and can be successful with. Texts at appropriate levels of complexity, web-based text work, and text downloaded from web-based services like ReadWorks.org can be used. Students can also read picture books that you have read often and they are familiar with, nonfiction texts on topics that they are investigating or interested in reading, chapter books, poems, songs, and any other text that students find engaging.

Practice tips: Create sentence strips for students, taken from the book they have read. They can practice rereading the sentence strips. You can also create sentences that contain recently taught skills and that are related to the book they have read independently. When students are ready, have them write a simple sentence that extends the story and then have them read it to themselves and to you. It's so powerful for students to apply their reading skills to writing; it helps them cement all their literacy skills.

WRITING ROUTINES

At the reading table, sometimes you are working on writing. Writing at the table serves two purposes. First, for emergent and early writers, you are guiding them to break the print-sound code and learn to spell words based on the sounds they hear and the corresponding letters and letter combinations. For more fluent writers, you will continue to help them encode multisyllabic words, and they will work to understand what letters or letter combinations represent increasing sophisticated words. Second, writing helps students with their comprehension. After discussing what a book or text is about, students can jot down notes and write sentences to reinforce their thinking.

ASSET LENS

Multilingual learners benefit from having a balance of reading and writing work at the reading table. Bates (2020) points out in her book *Interactive Writing* that students do the following during both reading and writing:

- Control directional movement
- Attend to the alphabetic principle
- Work on word-solving
- Monitor the message for meaning
- Read in a phrased and fluent manner

Encoding

Encoding is the skill that students use when spelling words. It is the writing practice of capturing the sounds they hear and spelling them. Encoding is not a routine as much as it is a skill. While writing, students are working independently and with support to hear sounds in words and write down the corresponding letters and letter combinations.

The benefits: When students first begin writing in English, they are working on the encoding of sounds; this is the building-on of phonics work. Students will encode words (as opposed to decode words already written) they want to write. We need to help them with encoding by providing time at the reading table to write about the texts that they are reading. Ensuring that multilingual learners know the sounds and letters and letter combinations that represent the sounds they hear empowers them to communicate their ideas and to write messages. Writing their ideas, thoughts, and the points they have learned is an excellent and authentic way for multilingual learners to use English for meaningful purposes.

How to do it: Perhaps the group decides to write a sentence about *Silly Sally* (Wood, 1994) after a shared reading of the book. The students may be motivated to sound out *silly* and spell it phonetically, which is perfectly fine. The important thing is not perfect spelling at first. What is important is that students are hearing the sounds in words, know the letters that represent those sounds, and work to write them out (Blevins, 2020). Sometimes at the reading table you may provide opportunities for writing dictated sentences, interactive writing, shared writing, or independent writing. Students will participate in these activities by encoding sounds into words. The key is to focus on what sounds the students hear and what letters they need to write to represent those sounds to express themselves.

> Ensuring that multilingual learners know the sounds and letters and letter combinations that represent the sounds they hear empowers them to communicate their ideas and to write messages.

Practice tip: Help students hear the sounds in words by connecting kinesthetics to sounds. Place one hand on the top of the opposite shoulder. Hold your hand flat, with your palm touching your arm. As you say a word, slide your hand down your arm. Tap the top of your shoulder when you say the word, and tap your wrist when you say the end of the word. Move with a sweeping motion. Encourage children to do the same so they can concentrate on the beginning and ending sounds at first. Help them focus on the medial sounds once they master the beginning and ending sounds. Have a sound chart handy of consonant blends, vowel pairs, *r*-controlled vowel, and digraphs to help students note the letter combinations for sounds they are hearing.

Guided Writing

In guided writing, you teach a specific writing point and then guide students to be able to do it on their own. You can teach any aspect of writing through guided writing. Hoyt (2016) points out the parallels between guided writing and guided reading. Both guided writing and guided reading are conducted in a small group setting and emphasize strategies. Both emphasize explicit teaching followed by students independently applying and reflecting upon the strategies that were taught. Both emphasize the teacher coaching the students to independence.

The benefits: You may engage students new to English, at the **entering** and **emerging** stages, and students at the **developing** level of language proficiency in guided writing. Multilingual learners are working through understanding how English works, and through guided writing, you can scaffold composing sentences, using academic vocabulary, and help with subject-verb agreement, along with other needs you notice in your formative assessment.

How to do it: In guided writing, you teach a specific writing point and then guide students to be able to do it on their own. For instance, you might want to focus on comprehension and have students write a sentence or two about the book that they have been reading at the table with you. Or you might focus on some aspect of writing, like stretching sounds in words to hear them and then write the appropriate letters. You would model how to stretch the sound and write the correct letter. Then you would encourage students to think of a few words (for students new to English) or a sentence (for students with more proficiency in English) they want to write and coach them as they stretch the words to hear the sounds and write the words down.

Guided Writing Lesson Framework

Step 1: Engagement in a topic—get students talking.

Step 2: Think aloud and share your thoughts; actively discuss the topic with students.

Step 3: Invite students to write. Teacher leans in and checks on students, providing support and help for students to be independent writers.

Step 4: Have students briefly share what they wrote.

Engagement

Brief shared-writing experience to help focus the purpose

Write to Practice

Students independently try out spelling words to communicate. The teacher provides specific feedback to help students as they listen to sounds in words in order to write.

Think Aloud and Active Discussion

Discuss with students their thinking about a topic and what they want to share and write. Provide coaching so that student's message is clear and is grammatically correct.

Brief Share

Students share out what they have written and discuss what they did to make sure their writing makes sense and communicates their ideas.

Dictated Writing

Dictated writing is to practice encoding, so it is a function of phonics instruction. Beyond the reading table, you can do dictated writing while working one-on-one with a child.

The benefits: For multilingual learners, dictated writing supports them as they work to integrate oral and print work. When you provide what they are to write, students don't have to think about the sentence construction and can instead focus on the sounds in the words, connect those sounds to the correct letter(s), and write them down. Dictations are not tests (Blevins, 2021); they are opportunities to practice encoding.

How to do it: First, you need to prepare one or more sentences that you want to say out loud that students will write. Say the sentences one at a time. Start by saying the entire sentence so that students can hear the "whole" of the sentence. Then, say the sentence more slowly, perhaps word by word as needed, to give students time to think through the words and how to spell the words. Third, during dictated writing, you will want to focus on the correct spelling of words and heavily support students to get the spelling correct. You can model if you need to if students get stuck. You can focus on students practicing their spelling. You can also introduce periods, capitals, and other punctuation marks, like question marks, so that students continue to develop their concepts of print while they are practicing the encoding of words (Gillingham & Stillman, 1997).

Interactive Writing

During interactive writing, students "share the pen" with the teacher. This gives the students the chance to practice their encoding skills while focusing on writing a meaningful message.

The benefits: Through interactive writing, students can work on encoding words with maximum support from the teacher. It also gives the students an opportunity to write a meaningful message about what is happening in class or what they might be investigating or reading. In negotiating meaningful texts and rereading them together, students gain valuable reading practice (Bates, 2020).

How to do it: The first step is to co-construct a message with the class. Keep the message to two to three sentences so that the message is a length that is engaging to students but not so long that they lose attention during the process. Second, you can begin by talking about what is the first word in the sentence or message and how that word might be written. Third, invite students to come up to the board or a chart and write the words you are spelling as part of the message (obviously in the order they appear in the sentence) or part of the word on the chart. All the students need to see the writing being constructed—charts work best. Fourth, check in with the class and see if they agree with how the word was written or spelled. The students who are watching can coach and support the student with the pen. After writing the entire message, finish by reading the message together.

Shared Writing

Shared writing is similar to interactive writing except that the teacher is scribing and the students are not sharing in the writing *down* of the words. At the reading table, you can conduct a shared writing with students after reading a book with them.

The benefits: Shared writing is a boon to oral language development and comprehension. Students new to English may only be able to share single words or simple phrases; however, you can model how those words and phrases connect in flowing sentences. During a shared writing, you can also reinforce concepts about print and the mechanics of writing, like capital letters and punctuation.

How to do it: You will first want to develop the message or information that will be written down. This is a good time to focus on oral language development and intellectually engage students in thinking about what they want to say (Gibson, 2020). Then while thinking aloud, you do all the writing, interacting with students to suggest what should be written down.

The steps to shared writing include the following:

1. Co-constructing the text with the class. Focus on oral language development and make the discussion meaningful by talking about a book that you read together at the reading table.

2. Writing the text out (Don't deliberately make mistakes; it can get confusing for students new to English, as they probably won't know how to "fix up" the writing).

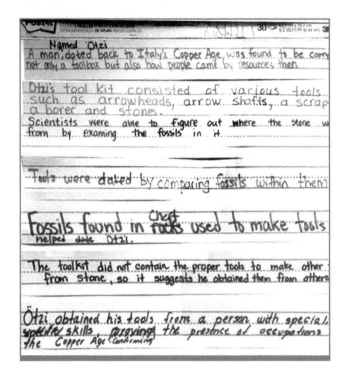

3. Rereading the writing with the class.

When you are working on a shared writing with students at the **expanding, bridging** and **reaching** levels, you are still scribing while thinking aloud or students are telling you what to write. With **bridging** and **reaching** levels, students may be ready to write in groups with different students being the scribe and the rest of the group of students providing ideas and thinking about what to write. The teacher does not have to be in control of how to compose the sentences. The students can take charge.

Use shared writing with students who have more developed language when

- You are facilitating a discussion about a text. You may want to model how to write about your thinking by writing on a whiteboard or chart, doing a think-aloud.

- You are scribing, suggesting sentence frames to help students get their ideas flowing.

- You are making your thinking or the students' thinking visible by pointing out what is going on, why you (or the students) are making the choices to put sentences together in a particular way.

- You are focused on meaning making.

Response Journals

Response journals give students an opportunity to respond to what they are reading and also provide a means for them to practice new skills. They may record their thinking about texts they have read. Their entries might include reflection on personal moments, poetry, fiction, and nonfiction texts. By having students organize their ongoing writing in response journals, you can easily see their growth and development over time.

The benefits: The use of response journals at the reading table develops self-evaluation, reflection, and awareness of knowledge and understanding for students acquiring English (Akhavan, 2006). Students at the **expanding** level will be writing with you at the reading table. However, students at the **bridging** and **reaching** levels may write with you at the reading table or may complete their writing away from the table.

For multilingual learners, the relevance of the writing task is key. When topics that students are reading about have purpose and interest for them, it is easier to write about thinking in relation to the texts. Brozo (2002) has talked about how boys are more motivated and engaged as readers when the topics are relevant. Focusing on high-interest topics is important for students who are growing and deepening their literacy skills. Gutherie and Barber (2019) suggest these steps in making reading relevant. These tips will help you select texts, and in turn, the writing students do in response will be relevant:

- Focus on real-world materials and topics

- Choose poignant topics

- Identify students' interest through interest inventories

- Determine linkages between students' lives and backgrounds and your community or the world at large

How to do it: You would first introduce the writing in the group and model how the writing would be accomplished or facilitate a discussion to prime the students' thinking to prepare them to write. Writing after reading should be to enhance and deepen comprehension, not prove to you that students read. Students at the **bridging** and **reaching** levels need to be writing in response to comprehension questions that get them thinking deeply. (See pages 81–83 to Chapter 4 for types of questions to ask.) Don't ask them who, what, when, and where questions: Focus instead on why and how questions to encourage students to think, to respond to text, and to go back and reread text to make connections within their thinking.

TYPES OF TEXTS TO USE

Knowing what type of texts to use with students at the reading table is part of preparing for lessons. Students will be more engaged in their writing and reading when we are intentional about the types of texts we use, but knowing how to select appropriate, high-interest texts can be a challenge.

With students at the **emerging** and **developing** stages, you aim for text that is engaging, simple to understand conceptually, and provides high success rates (Wharton-McDonald, 2011). However, students at the **expanding** and **bridging** levels will begin reading more complex text. Students at the **reaching** level will be accustomed to reading complex text and will be developing their skills in thinking about and analyzing deep and meaningful books, text, and materials.

Provide rich and engaging texts that amplify authors and stories from different cultures, races, and ethnicities. You can curate a library full of texts that provide a perspective on the immigrant experience as well an antibias focus. Resources for finding such books include the following:

- https://socialjusticebooks.org/

- https://teachinglatinamericathroughliterature.wordpress .com/

- http://richincolor.com/

- https://blog.leeandlow.com/

- https://indigosbookshelf.blogspot.com/

Use Interest Inventories

Almost two-thirds of students who are in the free and reduced-lunch programs do not have a plethora books of their own at home, so book access is important for students in wanting to read (Palmer, 1994; Pressely & Allington, 2015). When classrooms are rich in literature and authentic reading experiences, students are more motivated to read. Provide multiple types of texts in your classroom. Look for a balance between fiction and nonfiction, high-low readers, and novels for all ages. By giving an interest inventory, you can find out what topics, ideas, and subjects your students are interested in and provide texts on these subjects in your classrooms. The texts can be digital or in paper; what is important is access, availability, and honoring the need for quality texts to read. Make sure your students have access to a device and internet if you are making digital texts available for students.

Reading Interest Inventory Grades K-3

Student Name: _____ Date: _____

For each question, have students choose a face.

1. How do you feel about reading?

2. How does it feel when you are reading?

3. What type of book do you like to read? *(Have the books out and let students point.)*

   Easy chapter books   Poetry   Science fiction

   Fantasy/Fairy tales

   Nonfiction books   Mystery
   on topics you like

   What are those topics?

   Picture books   Picture books
   that are stories/fantasy   that are on real topics

4. Of these types of books (genres), which ones do you think you might like to read this year?

5. How can I help you with reading this year?

6. What goals do you have for yourself as a reader? What goal could you make?

Emojis credit: iStock.com/ringo sono

Reading Interest Inventory Grades 4–6

Student Name: _____ Date: _____

1. Do you like to read? Why or why not?

2. Have you read a book you loved? What was it about? What made you like it?

3. What genre of book do you usually like to read?

Realistic fiction	Historical fiction	Memoir
Graphic novels	Biography	Science fiction
Informational books	Fantasy	Humor/Comedy
Nonfiction books on topics you like	Thrillers	Poetry

What are those topics?

Dystopian	Mystery	Science fiction
Adventure	Picture books that are stories/fantasy	Picture books that are on real topics

4. Of these genres, which ones do you think you might like to read this year?

5. What makes or would make you a good reader?

6. What goals do you have for yourself as a reader? What goal could you make?

7. Do you read in your spare time? What do you usually do in your spare time?

Where to Find Books and Other Texts

You may be new to curating a set of books for your multilingual students to read, or you could be a pro. The tips and list that follow can give you direction or freshen up your current book/text library.

A word about leveled texts: Leveled texts are helpful at ensuring students are reading books within their zone of proximal development, but be careful! It is not helpful to pigeonhole a student into reading an exact level of text. Think of providing leveled texts in a range of levels. For instance, if assessment indicates a student is reading at a Level M, you could provide texts from L to O for the student to read and explore. Having options is important to keep students' motivation high and to ensure students are being stretched (Araim, 2016).

It is important to have a variety of text types on a multitude of subjects that reflect the diversity of the world to help students see themselves in text and validate their identities (Clark & Fleming, 2019).

Looking Ahead

I encourage you to revisit this chapter often! Again, it's your menu to graze as you get the hang of selecting routines for the reading table. The adage "variety is the spice of life" is apt because all students benefit from lively learning experiences that involve reading, writing, speaking, and listening and a wide array of routines. The routines in this chapter inform your teaching and learning throughout the literacy block. In selecting, you use your expertise and your intuitive sense of what students are ready for. The explicit teaching is always done in the context of meaningful reading and writing. In the next chapter, we look at how to use these options at the reading table to offer students engaging lesson sequences.

CHAPTER FOUR

Lesson Sequences

Let's start with a recap: In Chapter 1, you learned about the continuum of language acquisition. From the apprenticeship framework (page 31 in Chapter 2), you are equipped with the six steps that assure a supportive, engaging mix of teacher modeling and student practice at the reading table. In the previous chapter, I shared a menu of options—literacy skills and the routines for teaching them. Now, in this chapter, we do a deeper dive on how to select a few of them to make the 20 minutes together reading a text efficient, engaging, and intentional. You will see I tailor the sequences based on group composition and where students are on the language continuum.

DIFFERENTIATING INSTRUCTION

If you have a large number of multilingual learners in your class, you will be able to form reading groups aligned exactly to the reading needs of the students. For example, you might have a group for entering and emerging, another group for developing/bridging, and so on. The groups are flexible, meaning that from week to week you change membership in groups based on how each student is progressing. Or you might create several heterogeneous groups and work with multilingual students alongside of students who speak English as a heritage language or who are already fluent in English.

If, on the other hand, you only have a few multilingual learners in class, it may not be possible to have a group made up entirely of multilingual learners. In this scenario, you would place multilingual learners with students whose needs as readers are most aligned.

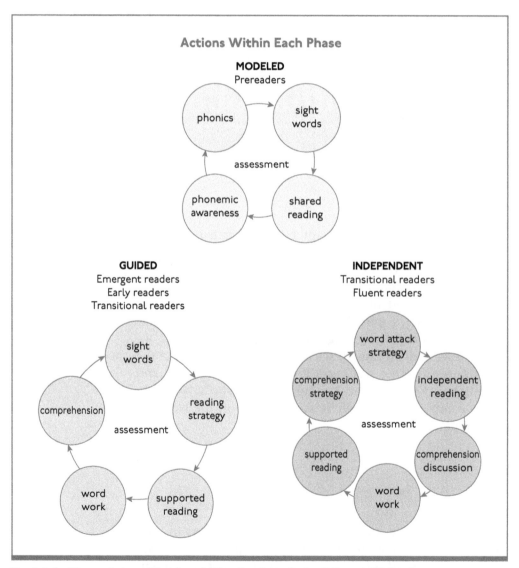

Reprinted with permission of Benchmark Education from the book *Remarkable Roads*.

What do I mean by needs as readers? If the students are reading at similar text levels or are working on the same decoding or comprehension strategies, those are examples of readers with similar needs.

Student need informs what you plan and what will be your instructional focus. You have a toolbox of scaffolds and supports you can use to guide student learning (see Chapter 3 for literacy scaffolds), and you will ramp up or ramp down various things based on the groups needs. For example, if I have a few multilingual learners and a couple of students whose first language is English and they all need/are ready to work on decoding multisyllabic words, I'd go with helping them strategize how to figure out how to say the word first, breaking the word into syllables and sounding them out. Then, I would help them learn the meaning of the words. Be sure to provide some supports and scaffolds to ensure the students acquiring English understand the language of the texts and conversations. Provide differentiated support to the one or two English language learners you may have in a small group. By doing this, you are providing strategic language support.

At the reading table, you are providing several scaffolds for students:

1. The smallness of the group provides support.

2. You have the opportunity to talk and explain, slow down your speech, and draw or diagram meanings of words.

3. You can even look up words on a device and show pictures or short videos.

4. You may also simplify vocabulary in order to explain concepts (Akhavan, 2006).

5. You can provide additional support with understanding the academic language and the academic register used in more sophisticated texts (Cazden, 2010).

Reading Experiences for Students at the Entering and Emerging Level

Students who are just beginning to acquire English need many different types of oral language experiences. They also need experiences with texts. They may not be able to read the texts, but by working with texts, they develop knowledge about literacy overall, about how English works, and the vocabulary in the texts. If they are young learners, they will be learning foundational skills—like concepts about print and phonemic awareness. If they are older learners and already know how to read in their heritage language, they will have the opportunity to explore the words and sentences and begin making connections between what they are starting to understand and the printed words on the page. We don't hold back literacy experiences just because a student is new to English.

You will be providing a plethora of oral language development opportunities at the reading table for students new to English and at all proficiency levels. Language acquisition builds from oral language development to written language development. However, you don't build oral language only at first; you weave the experiences together. So think enriching, exciting oral language development connected to letters and sounds, words, and texts.

During small group time, students who are just beginning to acquire English need the following:

- **Many different types of oral language experiences.** Enriching, exciting oral language development connected to letters and sounds, words, and texts.

- **Experiences with texts.** They may not be able to read the texts, but by working with texts, they develop knowledge about literacy overall, about how English works, and the vocabulary in the texts.

- **Foundational skills, like concepts about print and phonemic awareness.** They need to know how to decode and say words, as well as understand how words are put together.

- **Invitations to explore.** If they are older learners and already know how to read in their heritage language, they will have the opportunity to explore the words and sentences and think aloud, making connections between what they are starting to understand and the printed words on the page.

- **Knowledge building.** While students bring to the classroom abundant amounts of knowledge about the world, their background knowledge may differ from what they will experience in the texts they are reading with you. You need to spend time discussing the ideas and information in texts with students in order to build background knowledge (Collett & Dubetz, 2021).

Supports and Scaffolds for the Entering and Emerging Levels

There are a variety of things you can do with the students at the reading table:

1. Provide instruction that helps students to develop some understanding of what you are saying and what the text is about.

2. Use visuals (like pictures or drawings), video clips, and even use real items to show what words mean and what the text is discussing.

3. Point to things as you talk and draw pictures connecting your pictures to words that you say and write down.

4. Slow down what you are saying and repeat yourself often (Gibbons, 2009).

Students new to English may not be able to read the texts, but they can enjoy texts that you read, explore words, and work with foundational skills in reading. If they already know how to read in their heritage language, the foundational skills they will need to work on are the letters and sounds of English. For students able to read in their heritage language, ensure that you are giving them time to read in their heritage language so they can continue learning from reading and enjoying the reading process. While you can read aloud to students, shared readings can be very productive. Repeated readings of favorite texts provide time and space for students to read along with you. You can ask simple questions about the text, and students can respond with simple gestures or pointing.

Lessons for Students at Entering and Emerging Levels

You can focus on the following activities at the reading table for students at the entering and emerging proficiency levels.

These activities provide rich and varied opportunities to develop oral language and then expand to books and texts.

Entering: Vocabulary, read alouds, shared reading, phonemic awareness activities, phonics instruction, shared writing

Emerging: Sight words, vocabulary, phonemic awareness, phonics, read alouds, shared reading, choral reading, interactive and shared writing

CONNECTING THE LESSON SEQUENCE TO THE ACTIONS

Entering

I only have twenty minutes with the students at the reading table, so during the week, I will follow a sequence of what I am doing during small groups. Preferably, I am teaching small groups four to five days a week. A schedule for students new to English could include the following:

Each remaining chapter provides additional information about how to do each step in the sequence. What follows is an overview.

Day 1

Step 1: Students new to English need to learn to hear the sounds in English that make up words. They need to develop phonological awareness overall, which includes the ability to hear different words, as well as phonemic awareness, which is hearing each phoneme in words. For students new to English, at first when listening to English, they may not be able to hear individual words,

and words may flow together in unrecognizable sounds. Developing phonological awareness in English comes from the discussion of sounds and words but also many oral language experiences. You can develop phonological awareness for students by doing some of the activities in Chapter 6. Focus on students hearing the larger units of language such as words and sentences.

Step 2: Students new to English need opportunities to identify letters and the sounds connected to those letters. Depending on the students' heritage language, the formation of the English alphabet may be very different than what they have seen and known. They will need time to learn the formation of the letters and the name of each letters. For students who are already familiar with the Roman alphabet, they need to learn the 26 letters in English and the names for those letters.

Step 3: At the reading table, you can also spend quite a bit of time developing students' basic vocabulary in English.

You can do this in a variety of ways. For example, you can show students a picture or real item from around the classroom or things you have brought from home. Say the word of the item or thing depicted in the picture/item. Say it again slowly so students can hear the sounds in the word. Invite students to repeat the word and say it with you. Chat about the item or thing and use the word in a simple sentence. Invite students to repeat the word on their own. They can also repeat the sentence you say or make up their own sentence. You can also prepare pictures on cards and have a pocket chart and sentence strips handy. As you show students the pictures, you can hold up the picture, lay it out on a table in a small group, or put the picture in a pocket chart. Say the word the picture represents. If using a pocket chart, write the word and a sentence using the word on a sentence strip and put it in the pocket chart. Invite students to say the word and help you think of a sentence. You can also put the picture on the table and write the word on a whiteboard. Follow the same procedure, inviting students to say the word and stating a sentence using the word. Continue with additional words, but keep the number of new words introduced to a handful.

Word banks are very supportive for students acquiring language. It is important to have word banks all over your classrooms! Visuals make a big difference for students acquiring language. Create a word bank with the words you have introduced. Using chart paper, add words to the chart and draw or paste a picture representing the word next to the word. Organize words in a word bank around topics or themes like feelings, household items, food, parts of the body, adjectives, prepositions, and so forth.

Day 2

On Day 2 you will repeat work with sounds and with letters, and you will add in saying simple poems or singing simple songs. By engaging students in shared reading of simple poems, students can practice hearing sounds and words in English and associating those sounds and words with the print. You can also discuss the meaning of these simple poems and discuss the ideas in the poems. Spend lots of time discussing to ensure students understand. You may need to display a picture on a device from a website or draw pictures to help support student comprehension of the words in the poems and what the poems mean. You can also do these steps with simple songs like "Happy Birthday to You" or "Twinkle, Twinkle Little Star."

Day 3

On Day 3, you can repeat working with the sounds and words you started previously. You will also be adding in shared reading of a simple book or text. During shared reading, read the book to the students the first time through, stopping to discuss vocabulary that may be unknown to the students and talking about the overall meaning of the book or text. After the first read, invite students to choral read the book with you a second time. Invite students to share their thinking about the text in ways they are comfortable sharing.

For shared writing, guide the students to compose a sentence about the book, write it out for them or engage in an interactive writing, practicing sounding out the words with the students, helping to identify sounds and letters as much as possible.

(Continued)

(Continued)

ENTERING LESSON SEQUENCE

Day 1

Step 1: Work with sounds

Step 2: Work with letters

Step 3: Work with everyday vocabulary

Day 2

Step 1: Work with sounds

Step 2: Work with letters

Step 3: Read poems and sing songs

Day 3

Step 1: Work with sounds

Step 2: Work with letters

Step 3: Read a predictable story

Step 4: Shared writing

Work With Sounds	**Working With Letters**
Pictures representing sounds	Letter/Sound matching
Phoneme isolation	Letter name identification
Blending sounds	Blending
Phoneme substitution	Spelling CVC words
Adding and deleting sounds	
Substituting sounds	

Working With Everyday Vocabulary	**Work With Poems, Songs, Books**
Labeling objects in classroom	Singing songs
Working with small items and naming/labeling	Reciting poetry using visual charts with pictures
Practicing simple phrases	Previewing books
Total physical response (TPR)	Discussing illustrations
	Acting out songs, poems, simple stories

Shared Writing

Shared or interactive writing experience

EMERGING

For emerging students, I also want to capitalize on the twenty minutes I have with them in the small group. Much like the schedule that I planned for working with students new to English, I will differ what I do on different days of the schedule. Each remaining chapter provides additional information about how to do each step in the sequence. What follows is an overview.

A schedule I might use could be the following:

Day 1

Step 1: Work with sounds. Students will likely have developed some phonological awareness in English and would now be ready to work on phonemic awareness where they are practicing to isolate and manipulate sounds (phonemes). Chapter 6 provides numerous activities for phonemic awareness, and you can choose activities that match what your students need to practice with your guidance and implement them before working on decoding words. Once students are ready to practice decoding, ensure that you are introducing letters in the order suggested in Chapter 6. Choose an activity from the chapter and implement that activity at the table to help students learn the sounds each letter or letter grouping represents.

Step 2: Work with sight words. Learning sight words gives students opportunities to memorize and recognize on sight some of the most common words in English. Having a strong sight word vocabulary helps students with fluency and provides some mental relief from sounding out every

word in a sentence (Fry & Rasinski, 2007). Working with sight words involves practicing looking at the word, saying the word, writing the word down on a whiteboard or in a journal, and also noticing the word parts to commit the word to memory. For example, if I were to teach the sight word *the,* I would discuss how the digraph *th* feels in our mouth when we say it and I would discuss how the *e* sounds when pronouncing *the.* We would practice saying it a few times and write it out several times on a whiteboard so students could become familiar with the word and begin to know it on sight.

Step 3: Shared reading of predictable text. Students need numerous opportunities to be successful with text, and shared reading provides ample support. During shared reading, read the book to the students the first time through, stopping to discuss vocabulary that may be unknown to the students and talking about the overall meaning of the book or text. After the first read, invite students to read the book with you a second time. They may have memorized the words or just be repeating after you and not yet reading the text; this is fine. They are learning to associate the words they are saying with the print. Invite students to share their thinking about the text in ways they are comfortable sharing.

Day 2

Step 1: Work with sounds—focus on decoding. This is the day students will use their knowledge of sounds to read a decodable text. To prepare them to

(Continued)

(Continued)

read a decodable, practice what the students have been working on during Day 1. Introduce any new sound as necessary and practice reading some of the words from the decodable book in isolation. Perhaps write the words from the book on a whiteboard and practice sounding them out and saying the words together.

Step 2: Shared reading decodable text. Focus on how the sounds work together to make words and then sentences; decodables, while purposeful, have language limits. Also focus on discussing the text to build oral language. Reinforce students for their efforts to figure out what the words are and encourage them to reread sentences for fluency.

Step 3: Shared reading from poem or choral reading/singing from a song book. Make sure to discuss the text to build oral language. End the session with a group reading of a text that students have read often together, perhaps something previously read during whole group instruction. This can be a song or poem written out on a chart. You can point to the words while students sing the lyrics or as they read the poem. Choose a poem with a beat so that students can use the rhythm to help them with the reading. Students may very likely not be reading but can follow along with your hand as they are learning to associate what they are saying with the printed words.

Day 3

Step 1: Work with sounds—focus on writing words. Reinforce the sounds that you have introduced on previous days—however, now, use those sounds to build words. Using magnetic letters, have students make words and then write them out on whiteboards. Begin by saying the target word.

Encourage students to listen for the sounds in those words and write the corresponding letters. Ensure that students (not you) are mentally processing what sounds they hear, and support them while they identify the correct letter(s) that make the sound.

Step 2: Work on vocabulary you will use in the sentences. Students at the emerging level will be ready to enhance their vocabulary. They may be ready for more sophisticated words about subjects you are studying in class or words that change meaning— like adjectives or different verb tenses. Introduce the words you will be using to have students write sentences.

Step 3: Dictate sentences using the vocabulary words. Choose a simple sentence that you believe students would be successful writing on their own after practicing the words and listening for sounds in the words in order to spell them. First say the sentence, then count the words in the sentence so students know how many words they are going to write, and then guide students to write the sentence by restating each word slowly.

Step 4: Draw a picture and write a sentence about the story from Day 1 or Day 2 using a sentence frame. You can extend the sentence writing by returning to a book you read earlier in the week and encouraging students to write a sentence or two about the book. Focus on comprehension of the book's or text's meaning. If needed, provide a sentence frame for students to use. Some sentence frames can include the following:

- The main idea is
- The story is about
- The main character is
- The problem was
- The facts are

EMERGING LESSON SEQUENCE

Day 1

Step 1: Work with sounds

Step 2: Work with sight words

Step 3: Shared reading of predictable text

Day 2

Step 1: Work with sounds—focus on decoding

Step 2: Share reading decodable text

Step 3: Share reading from poem or choral reading/singing from a songbook, making sure to discuss the text to build oral language

Day 3

Step 1: Work with sounds—focus on writing words

Step 2: Work on vocabulary you will use in the sentences

Step 3: Dictate sentences using the vocabulary words

Step 4: Draw a picture and write a sentence about the story from Day 1 or Day 2 using a sentence frame

---

Work With Sounds	**Working With Sight Words**
Blending sounds	Decode word
Phoneme substitution	Play games with words
Adding and deleting sounds	Write words
Substituting sounds	Create word lists
	Work on fluent reading of words

Working With Vocabulary	**Shared Reading**
Discuss book pictures	Read and sing songs together
Practice simple phrases	Reciting poetry using visual charts
Total Physical Response (TPR)	Read books together with teacher reading aloud
Create word banks	
Use sentence frames	

Develop Oral Language	**Guided Writing**
Encourage speaking in simple phrases	Model writing sentences
Asking yes/no questions	Compose sentences together
Ask for ideas	Guide students to write words

READING EXPERIENCES FOR STUDENTS AT THE DEVELOPING LEVELS

In this next set of lesson sequences, notice that once students are beyond the emerging level of English language acquisition, you **add in choral reading**. Students can read more difficult text together, supporting one another or with you leading the reading as a model.

- **Add in independent reading.** Students need maximum time to practice reading skills they are developing in order to become strong and fluent readers. The more they read, the stronger readers they will become.

- **Cut back on shared reading.** You may be doing shared reading during whole group instruction at another time of day, so you can include it at the reading table but less often; this rule of thumb is only for the work at the reading table. The reason for this is you will begin expanding beyond oral language development about texts and add in literacy experiences where students begin working learning and acquiring language by reading more extensively and working with texts.

Lessons for Students at the Developing Level of Language Proficiency

Developing: Sight words, vocabulary, phonemic awareness, phonics, shared reading, choral reading, independent reading, comprehension, writing

CONNECTING THE LESSON SEQUENCE TO THE ACTIONS
Developing

Groups will still be about twenty minutes long, and there will be more balance between the amount of time between the teaching (the I do) and the time that the students spend reading on their own (the You do).

Day 1

Step 1: On the first day with a book, start with sight word review and/or teach decoding skills focusing on letter-sound combinations and how to break words into syllables to decode.

Step 2: Next, introduce the new book, preteaching the most important two to three vocabulary words that the students need in order to understand the text (most words need to be taught during the read, and that will be discussed in Chapter 6). Discuss the words, amply focusing on ensuring students understand what the words mean. Give a synopsis of the book and do a book walk.

Step 3: Have students read the book on their own. This is independent reading with you coaching.

Step 4: After reading, discuss what students thought of the books and review the key vocabulary in context. Read the sentences where the words appear and discuss what the students think about the words' meanings.

Day 2

Step 1: On the second day with the book, begin with a quick talk about the book, reminding students of what the key vocabulary words mean.

Step 2: Students read the books again (or part of the book) and stop and talk about additional vocabulary words that may need to be reviewed. Review the teaching point that you focused on during Day 1 with the book.

Step 3: Prompt students in a guided writing with the book (see Chapter 6 for how-tos). They can write in a journal focused on a reading comprehension strategy, or you can work on dictated sentences using one or two of the new vocabulary words.

(Continued)

(Continued)

 ## DEVELOPING LESSON SEQUENCE

Day 1

Step 1: Sight word review

Step 2: Teach decoding skills or comprehension strategy

Step 3: Introduce new book

Step 4: Read

Step 5: Discuss

Day 2

Step 1: Discuss book/review key vocabulary

Step 2: Read book again

Step 3: Guided writing

Working With Sight Words

Decode word

Dictate words

Say it, Stretch it, Write it

Create word lists

Work on fluent reading of words

Working With Vocabulary

Discuss book pictures

Practice simple phrases

Create word banks

Use sentence frames

Guided Writing

Think, plan, write

Guide students to write sentences between three and ten words

Focus on spelling

Teaching Point

Word solving—decoding

Word solving for meaning—discuss

Retelling

Main idea and details

Character, plot, setting

Reading Experiences for Students at the Bridging and Reaching Levels

Students at the bridging and reaching levels need to experience a higher level of interactive instruction and discussion, so you will need to **balance when you are teaching skills and strategies directly and when you are facilitating conversations** (Cummins, 1984; Tharp, 1997). The meeting at the reading table should feel somewhat like a social gathering around literacy discussions.

Peer work. Students at the bridging level can learn from interactions with peers and with you. They may be more watchful at first and then engage more often as they learn to discuss text together (Genesee & Riches, 2006).

Questions that invite thinking/sharing. As you read texts, purposefully look for ways to draw out students' experiences. These discussions leverage multilingual learners' diverse sociocultural backgrounds (Genesee & Riches, 2006). Through learning by talking, students can bring new perspectives and different insights into the examination of text. It can be quite helpful to provide supports for these discussions, like providing sentence frames for appropriate interaction with peers about text.

Sentence starters for literary conversations

"I noticed that . . ."

"I disagree, I think that . . ."

"In the text it says . . . ; this makes me think of . . ."

"I also noted . . ."

Like . . . , I am seeing connections between . . . and . . ."

Lessons for Students at the Bridging Levels

You can focus on the following activities at the reading table for students at the expanding and bridging proficiency levels. These activities provide rich and varied opportunities to develop academic language, both orally and in writing.

> **Bridging and Reaching:** Oral language development, vocabulary, comprehension, close reading, independent reading, shared writing, independent writing, word work, spelling

CONNECTING THE LESSON SEQUENCE TO THE ACTIONS

Bridging

The meeting at the reading table for students at the bridging level can last more than twenty minutes because of the length of some of the comprehension discussion you may have. However, only lengthen your sessions at the reading table if the students who are not at the reading table have purposeful work to do and you can still fit all your groups into the schedule. Otherwise, you will need to keep the groups to twenty minutes and stretch the activities across additional days.

Day 1

Step 1: Introduce text, previewing the text.

Step 2: Teach important vocabulary from the text.

Step 3: Students read a page or two.

Step 4: Discuss comprehension focusing on a three-read sequence.

(In a three-read, students survey the text on a first read [you did that together in Step 1], then read the text on a second read quickly to understand what the text is about or saying, and finally, after a third read, discuss the deep meaning of the text, making connections between ideas, points, and deeper meaning.)

Step 5: Discuss notes for the reading journal and model using sentence frames as needed.

Step 6: Assign independent reading of the same text.

Day 2

Step 1: Discuss reading that was assigned, focusing on unknown vocabulary and comprehension.

Step 2: Teach any unknown vocabulary.

Step 3: Teach a comprehension strategy.

Step 4: Practice the comprehension strategy together by reading part of the text.

Step 5: Review reading journal expectations and assign independent reading of the text.

Day 3

Step 1: Discuss reading that was assigned, focusing on unknown vocabulary and comprehension.

Step 2: Teach any unknown vocabulary by referring to the vocabulary use in context.

Step 3: Shared writing of ideas and concepts from the text; the shared writing can be a variety of writing types. See the comprehension chapter for ideas, Chapter 9.

Step 4: If students have finished reading the text, discuss overall themes, ideas, and/or meaning of the text and move onto a new text in the future. If the book or text is not finished, repeat Steps 1 and 2 until the book/text is completed.

CONSTRUCTIVE CONVERSATION

What connections can I make?

What is clear or confusing?

What is the text mainly about?

How do I know?

Read to understand the text:

What is happening in the text?

What language do I need to clarify?

What do I remember about what I read?

(Continued)

(Continued)

BRIDGING LESSON SEQUENCE

Day 1

Step 1: Introduce and preview text

Step 2: Vocabulary preteach

Step 3: Read

Step 4: Discuss comprehension

Step 5: Write

Step 6: Assign independent reading

Day 2

Step 1: Discuss for comprehension

Step 2: Teach unknown vocabulary

Step 3: Teach comprehension strategy

Step 4: Practice comprehension strategy

Step 5: Write in reading journal

Day 3

Step 1: Discuss reading

Step 2: Teach unknown vocabulary

Step 3: Shared writing about text

Step 4: Discuss text

Working With Vocabulary

Discuss sentences around the word

Practice use in sentences and phrases

Create word banks

Use sentence frames

Write About Reading

Write focusing on a comprehension strategy

Comprehension Strategies

Predict

Ask and answer questions

Summarize main idea and details

Infer, using text structures and text features

Visualize

Compare and contrast

WAYS TO SUPPORT STUDENTS AT THE REACHING LEVEL

Students who have developed high levels of proficiency in English may seem to not need support to comprehend text or develop their reading skills. What they do need support in is continued growth as readers. You can encourage them to read more. Additional reading time has a positive effect on over-all reading ability for English language learners (Shanahan & Beck, 2006). Tudor and Hafiz (1989) conducted a study where they provided one hour of additional reading time for English language learners. The teacher met with the students and provided support with unknown vocabulary. The students showed strong gains in their reading ability in English.

You can do a *book flood* from time to time in your classroom, where students are given access to many, many books and allowed to read books for the pure enjoyment of reading for twenty to thirty minutes. During a book flood, students can self-select books and spend time reading books of their choosing, changing out books as they need to in order to sustain interest. Sustained time reading increases students literacy levels in English and helps them become better readers overall (Elley, 1991).

READING EXPERIENCES FOR STUDENTS AT THE REACHING LEVEL

Students at the reaching level will be able to work effectively with peers whose heritage language is English. Students at the reaching level have developed their English language proficiency to a point where they may no longer be considered "English language learners" and indeed might be bilingual and biliterate. However, when students are at a near-native level of English proficiency, they will still need the following:

- **Support in integrating.** Students at the reaching proficiency level will be ready to fully integrate into the classroom. It is important to set them up for success by pairing students up who work well together and can support each other. These can be small groups that involve multilingual learners and students whose heritage language is English. Remember, when multilingual students feel supported and emotionally safe, they will be able to focus on what they are learning and how they are communicating and not be worried about ridicule or embarrassment.

- **Book groups.** Students can meet in groups reading novels they are interested in or reading nonfiction texts on topics of interest.

- **Inquiry work.** Students may be studying particular topics in order to understand topics or interesting ideas deeply. Perhaps students are trying to solve a real-world problem (like recycling in the school cafeteria) or researching a topic for an informative report.

- **Vocabulary work.** You may need to meet with students at the reaching level once in a while to discuss academic language registers and vocabulary that may be new to them. However, I find that these conversations also benefit students whose heritage language is English, so you don't necessarily need to meet with the students at the reaching level separately.

- **One-on-one meetings.** All students benefit from conferring with you, of course. For reaching level students, meet from time to time for deep discussion about concepts that relate to readings they are involved in.

Looking Ahead

Now we turn to Part II of this book; beginning on the next page, you are entering the land of Teaching Ideas to use at the reading table! These are the specific activities you can select for the lesson sequences for Day 1, Day 2, and Day 3.

Lessons for Students at the Reaching Level of Language Proficiency

> **Reaching:** Vocabulary, comprehension, close reading, independent reading, writing, and discussion about what was read

Reaching Level

The guided book club lesson is very similar to when students run an independent book club on their own. With the guided club, however, you will want to facilitate it. For example, you convene the book club and then reconvene it at a later time (maybe a different day). Students can go off and meet without you, but you will sometimes want to have them focus on a strategy. If you are focusing on a strategy, you follow the six steps outlined here. Fluent readers still need strategy lessons as they read harder texts and encounter more difficult vocabulary. The steps to a strategy lesson are similar to the steps in a transitional guided reading lesson.

Step 1: Set purpose for reading

The first step to a fluent reader strategy lesson is to help students set a purpose for reading, check in with readers, and discuss difficult vocabulary. You may discuss a comprehension strategy that the students have been working on, or you discuss a difficult vocabulary word that students encountered in a text. Once the discussion is done, it is really important that you guide students to set their own purpose for reading. You might ask questions like, "How could you use that strategy today while reading?" or "In what ways do you think the strategy will help you today?" You want the students to own the purpose before they dive into the book.

Step 2: Introduce the book

Next, you can do a short book or text preview and invite students to read. You can give the students a short synopsis of the book, or section of the text, where they are going to practice a strategy.

Note: If you are working with guided book clubs and you just want to focus on the reading and are not concerned about teaching a strategy, here are the steps to follow. Remember, in this type of lesson, the reading happens BEFORE students come to the reading table:

1. Review what was read thus far and discuss any difficult vocabulary

2. Review/Discuss the book (or part of the book if students didn't read the whole book)

3. Write about the reading

4. Word study

5. Set purpose for reading

Step 3: Teach comprehensive strategy

Teach a comprehension strategy that you want students to focus on while they are reading the book or reading a section of the book. Discuss the strategy and model it for the students so they are clear on how they will be using the strategy while they are reading.

Step 4: Students read the book

Invite students to read. Again, as in transitional guided reading, students are in charge of their own reading. They are reading on their own, at their own pace. You can lean in with a student or two and ask them to read aloud to you for a short while in order to record notes or assess the students' fluency or miscues. Or students can leave the table and find their own spot to read.

Step 5: Students discuss the book

Once students have read the book, section of the book, or selection of text, reconvene at the table and discuss the book. During this step, you want the students to be in charge of the book discussion. You can launch the discussion, but invite students to own the discussion, jumping in with examples from the text, offering ideas or counter ideas to their peers thinking about the text. It is this type of rich book discourse that encourages students to think beyond surface level meaning of the text and provides them opportunities to practice comprehension strategies. Reinforce the comprehension strategy that you just modeled for the students.

Step 6: Students write about their reading

After the book discussion, students can write about their reading. When students write about their reading, they record their thinking about the book discussion, share how they used a comprehension strategy, or share their thoughts about what is happening in the book or text. You can pose an idea for the writing, but relate it back to the discussion and focus on writing that will help students deepen their comprehension of what they are reading. Have students quickly share out what they wrote in their reading journals; you can then retell or summarize overall and set a purpose for reading before the group meets again.

 REACHING LESSON SEQUENCE

Day 1

Step 1: Set purpose for reading

Step 2: Introduce book

Step 3: Teach comprehension strategy

Step 4: Read

Step 5: Discuss

Step 6: Write about their reading

Working With Vocabulary

Discuss sentences around the word

Practice use in sentences and phrases

Create word banks

Use sentence frames

Write About Reading

Write focusing on a comprehension strategy

Comprehension Strategies

Predict

Ask and answer questions

Summarize main idea and details

Infer using text structures and text features

Visualize

Compare and contrast

Reading Purpose

Explore topics

Understand theme and human experience

Connect ideas together

Answer questions

Make meaning from text

Teaching Ideas

TEACHING IDEAS

Developing Reading Skills

- As you plan your small-group lessons each week, you can use the rest of this book to find the just-right activities.

- Use the lesson sequences offered in Chapter 4 to tailor instruction to your students' proficiency stages—these sequences give you the "basic architecture" of your 20 minutes of instruction.

- I encourage you to take your cues from what you are seeing your students doing day-to-day! You are continually evaluating how they are grasping what you teach; you will know when to ramp up a particular skill area and when to move on.

CHAPTER FIVE

Oral Language Development

iStock.com/SolStock

"Toad pulled all the covers over his head," Pramila says softly. "So maybe he's sad?"

"Yes, and his friend Frog helps him. He gets him outside into the sun," adds Santosh.

The teacher nods her head in agreement and says, "I am going to reread this part. 'Toad blinked in the bright sun. "Help!" said Toad. "I cannot see anything." "Don't be silly," said Frog.'" The teacher leans toward the four students at the reading table, encouraging them as she says, "Why can't Toad see?"

"He has a blanket over his head!" Jessica responds, pointing at the illustration. "Silly!"

The other students laugh. The teacher quotes from the text, "'Don't be silly . . .' I'm going to write this expression on the whiteboard, because it's a good one to understand."

Talking, thinking about books, and discussing ideas—all these endeavors fall under the umbrella of oral language. Building understandings by speaking is a boon to multilingual students, but maybe more importantly, talk makes what is happening at the reading table *interesting*. You may notice that I didn't include "oral language development" as a menu item on the lesson sequences in Chapter 4. This is because oral language development is the foundation for *all* the work that is happening at the reading table: supporting spelling, vocabulary, word work, comprehension, and writing about reading.

COMMON CHALLENGES

What comes to mind when we consider oral language development for multilingual learners? Following are some common responses from educators across the grades.

Primary grades: Opportunities for oral language through play and storybook reading, singing, and poetry reading.

Intermediate grades: Opportunities for students to talk and listen to each other and to the teacher to pick up basic words.

Upper grades: Opportunities that invite students who are new to English to listen and speak.

Now, there is nothing wrong with any of these responses, but the more you know about teaching multilingual learners, the more you sense that these statements sell multilingual students short. Taken as a whole, they reflect a narrow understanding of oral language and what it can do. The truth is, oral language development goes beyond helping students new to English begin to understand what is being said and guiding them to say simple phrases (Carnegie Council on Adolescent Literacy, 2010).

Perhaps the greatest roadblock for multilingual learners is a classroom that is too quiet. Multilingual learners need many,

many opportunities to interact with other students, and all these opportunities help them acquire language (Gamez, 2009). Unfortunately, multilingual students often don't get the chance to talk and listen often to one another as they share their thinking about the text and the content area topics. Passive learning environments (when the teacher talks a lot and students listen a lot; or when the teacher asks questions and one student answers with just a short utterance) don't give students the robust experiences they need to use language and develop proficiency (Gamez, 2009; García & Malkin, 1993).

What Students Need

As you dip in and out of this chapter to select instructional ideas, use the words I've highlighted in bold as a quick reminder of the breadth of opportunities multilingual learners need.

Oral language development in its fullest sense includes the **listening and speaking** domains of English language acquisition (see Chapter 5, about listening and speaking). Oral language development also occurs through **vocabulary discussion** based on reading and on watching content-area videos. **Interpersonal communication through talk,** which is especially key early on, stokes motivation and students' grasp of colloquial English.

As students progress into the intermediate and upper elementary grades, oral language development requires explicit instruction in **vocabulary and grammar**, which involves **purposeful conversations** about topics and texts that bolster **academic vocabularies** (Kieffer, 2012). **Read alouds** and **deep-thinking read alouds** scaffold multilingual learners' abilities to integrate listening, grammar, and vocabulary skills to comprehend.

> "Passive learning environments
> . . . don't give students
> the robust experiences
> they need."

ATTRIBUTES OF DYNAMIC ORAL LANGUAGE INSTRUCTION

When oral language development is dynamic, it can be heard throughout the day beyond the reading table. It is an integral part of content-area learning and writing instruction too. Another hallmark of effective oral language development is that multilingual learners have many opportunities to talk at all phases of learning to read.

In reading instruction, you will have the opportunity to provide a plethora of oral language development opportunities for students at all language proficiency levels. Language acquisition builds from oral language development to written language development. However, you don't build oral language only at first; you weave the experiences together (Lightbrown & Spada, 1990). Therefore, it makes sense for us to mine the riches of the texts we read with students. Ask yourself, *How can I squeeze the most out of this story or poem or informational text to develop oral language*? You take what is most enriching, exciting, and engaging in a text and use it as a springboard for your oral language work. Depending on the stage of your readers, you can plan connections to letters, vowel combinations, assonance. You can connect to vocabulary, concepts, thinking aloud how to infer—the possibilities are endless. And the beauty of discussion is that it's inherently responsive to the learners; you can authentically ebb and flow between high teacher support to low teacher support.

> "You don't build oral language only at first; you weave the experiences together."

Oral Language Development and Skilled Reading

Researcher Hollis Scarborough conceptualized skilled reading as a rope (Scarborough, 2001). It's been rediscovered recently, as it so clearly reminds us that for students to have strong comprehension, they must have strong language comprehension and word recognition (Blevins, 2021). Oral language development is the lynchpin in all of it.

In the following graphic, notice the skills in the upper and lower strands. Notice that the **word-recognition** strands (phonological awareness, decoding, and sight recognition of familiar words) work together as the reader becomes accurate, fluent, and increasingly automatic with repetition and practice.

Concurrently, the **language-comprehension** strands (background knowledge, vocabulary, language structures, verbal reasoning, and literacy knowledge) reinforce one another and then weave together with the word-recognition strands to produce a skilled reader.

ASSET LENS

Students' vocabulary knowledge and language structures need to be developed purposefully as students work with texts (Scarborough, 2001). It's important to appreciate, however, that while students bring abundant amounts of knowledge about the world, their background knowledge may differ than what they will experience in the texts they are reading with you. Therefore, it's crucial for you to spend time discussing the ideas and information in texts with students to build background knowledge.

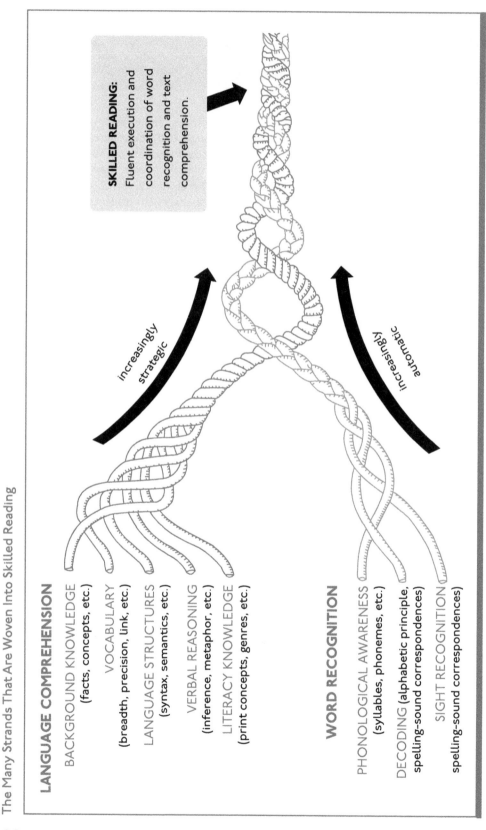

LANGUAGE COMPREHENSION

BACKGROUND KNOWLEDGE
(facts, concepts, etc.)

VOCABULARY
(breadth, precision, link, etc.)

LANGUAGE STRUCTURES
(syntax, semantics, etc.)

VERBAL REASONING
(inference, metaphor, etc.)

LITERACY KNOWLEDGE
(print concepts, genres, etc.)

WORD RECOGNITION

PHONOLOGICAL AWARENESS
(syllables, phonemes, etc.)

DECODING (alphabetic principle,
spelling–sound correspondences)

SIGHT RECOGNITION
spelling–sound correspondences)

*increasingly
strategic*

*increasingly
automatic*

SKILLED READING:
Fluent execution and
coordination of word
recognition and text
comprehension.

Source: Scarborough, H. S. (2001).

Early Oral Language Development

Early oral language development is connected to how well students read in later grades, particularly their reading abilities up to third grade (Cats et al., 2006; Kieffer, 2012; Melby-Lervåg & Lervåg, 2014). Oral language development means that students can produce or comprehend spoken language, including the vocabulary used and grammar (NELP, 2008). For multilingual students, oral language development in their heritage language is particularly essential for students' ability to read in English as well as being able to read in their heritage language (Cummins, 1979; Gutierrez et al., 2010).

Later Oral Language Development

Students need oral language development as they continue into the **bridging** and **reaching** levels of language acquisitions to continue their vocabulary and grammar development (August et al., 2005). It is also a necessity for rapid growth in reaching achievement in later grades (Chall, 1983; Snow et al., 2005). Keep in mind, this is not *you* talking only; it is about *all of you* talking about books and texts at the reading table together. Oral language development needs to be sustained over time (Carnegie Council on Adolescent Literacy, 2010).

Three tiers: For example, the words that vocabulary and reading researchers Beck et al. (2013) label as Tier I words are mostly basic words that are part of everyday life. These are words like *table, chair, baby,* and *happy.* Beck et al. (2013) suggest that these words rarely need instruction. This is true for students whose heritage language is English, but multilingual students do need instruction in Tier I and as well at Tier II and Tier III words as they continue acquiring language. Tier II words are words found across content areas, like *supervision, exploration,* and *synthesis.* Tier III words are content, or domain, area words that connect to English, science, mathematics, and social studies.

Oral language development later also includes students' listening comprehension. Listening comprehension requires students to integrate vocabulary and grammatical knowledge. These two skills have a strong relationship with later reading comprehension (Kieffer, 2012). In other words, what students learn in vocabulary and grammar through authentic and purposeful conversations about what they read with you and

> "Early oral language development is connected to how well students read in later grades."

their peers has an influence on how well they read in middle school and beyond.

BEGIN WITH LISTENING COMPREHENSION

"Listening comprehension requires students to integrate vocabulary and grammatical knowledge."

Students being able to talk and communicate well means that they need to understand each other; they must listen and know what is being said (Gottlieb, 2006). This doesn't mean that you spend lots of time reading aloud; this means you provide many opportunities for students to talk and listen. You don't want the time at the reading table to be quiet. Foster listening comprehension by encouraging revoicing, repeating, reasoning, adding on, and waiting.

Supporting Oral Language

Revoicing: Repeating all or some of what a student said. Use this move if what was said was unclear. Ask the student to verify correctness. Students can revoice each other's communication, or you can revoice students' communications.

Repeating: Ask one student to restate what another student said. The original speaker can confirm correctness.

Reasoning: Asking students to apply their reasoning to another person's idea, providing evidence and meaning to their reasons.

Adding on: Prompting students for further participation. This move increases student engagement in a nonthreatening manner.

Waiting: Building in wait-time in order to give students time to gather their thoughts and prepare an answer. You can ask students to pause their conversation and wait for each other, and you can pause your own conversation and give students time.

Focus on Grammar

It is extremely important that grammar is taught in context, not through drills and worksheets. Grammar is part of oral language development (August, 2003; Tong et al., 2008). Grammar isn't about teaching a strict division of language rules, as this can make students feel anxious and tongue-tied (McKay, 2006). Grammar is about talking about how sentences are constructed and gentle correction through conversation about the correct way to say something.

Focus on grammar in the following ways:

Revoicing: Repeating all or some of what a student said but saying the sentence with correct grammar as a model, then pause and explain how you corrected the sentence. For example, if the student says, "I goed to the library at lunch and choosed a book." You could revoice by saying, "Oh, so during lunch recess you went to the school library and chose a book? Great! I said *went* instead of *goed* because that is the past tense form. I said *chose* instead of *choosed* because that is the past tense form. I am SO happy though that you tried out the *-ed* endings like we talked about last week. Great work!"

Modeling: In the preceding example, I could help make the language visual for multilingual learners by writing the two sentences out on a whiteboard. I could circle or underline the correct form of past tense. When doing this, I would be careful to scaffold the use of the past tense forms of both verbs. I could also list out a few other verbs and their past tense form so we could practice quickly as a group.

. . . .

"It is extremely important that grammar is taught in context, not through drills and worksheets."

. . . .

Focus on Vocabulary

When students talk, they need something to talk about! I address explicit vocabulary instruction in Chapter 7. Here, we focus on learning words in the context of oral language development (August, 2003; Tong et al., 2008). During conversations at the reading table, reinforce the vocabulary you are teaching (see Chapter 9) through review and repetition play. Playing with words is intrinsically important for helping students talk and listen to you and to each other (López-Jiménez, 2010).

Focus on repetition and word play by doing the following:

- Pointing out repeating vocabulary in text

- Stopping and highlighting new words and saying them repeatedly (not rotely but in a fun way—make up a rhyme!)

- Stop and examine a new word; give the definition in a way that is understandable to students and talk about how the word is used in the text

- Write words encountered in text on a whiteboard, draw pictures about the word, talk with students about the word, and have them write it on their whiteboards also

- Invite students to write a sentence with the new words (Laufer & Hulstijn, 2001)

- Invite students to talk about what the word meaning makes them think about (López-Jiménez, 2010)

INTEGRATING LISTENING, GRAMMAR, AND VOCABULARY INSTRUCTION

Bring together listening, grammar, and vocabulary in conversations you have with students about their reading. Multilingual students often lack opportunities to put the vocabulary they know and the new vocabulary they are learning into a meaningful context (Shin & Crandall, 2013). Asking questions and leading conversations provide these opportunities. For example, my students and I were reading *Ready to Fight the Wind* by F. Isabel Campoy—there is a sentence that says, "in a way only she can do," referring to equal pay for equal work. So I pointed the sentence out to students and asked them to reread it. I asked, "What do you notice? How does that sentence do such a great job of showing us how Lorena felt about her brother getting paid more than she did for the same work?

Use a Continuum of Questioning Complexity

Begin by thinking of different types of questions you can ask. Degener and Berne (2016) devised a Continuum of Questioning Complexity that includes six levels. You can vary the type of questions you ask students about their reading based on these different levels.

- Level 1 is word-level decoding: Ask students how to say a word when reading.

- Level 2 is word-level vocabulary: Ask students what they think a word means, or discuss the word together.

- Level 3 is sentence-level comprehension: Discuss with students the meaning of sentences and how the sentences are constructed.

- Level 4 is cumulative comprehension: Chunk text into parts and stop and discuss what the section of text means, highlighting unknown vocabulary and explaining, then have students share their own thoughts about the words and text.

- Level 5 is critical consideration: Invite students at the bridging and reaching levels of language proficiency into a lengthier conversation about what they read, asking them to evaluate the text or weigh in on the author's meaning or intent.

- Level 6 is discerning greater meaning: Provide the opportunity for students, particularly those at the bridging and reaching levels of language proficiency, to make text-to-world and text-to-text connections, converging ideas together.

DEEP-THINKING READ ALOUDS

A read aloud is an opportunity for a co-constructed social conversation. The social co-construction of meaning happens when new information is integrated into what the students already know (Sailors et al., 2016). While most of the time at the reading table will be spent with students reading independently, there is time for read alouds *if* the focus of the read aloud is oral language comprehension. The read aloud is a powerful way to practice language with students. Often when students participate in deep thinking, ask questions of the text, and make claims about a text, they are making inferences. Notice how you can prompt for inferences in Step 2 of the Deep-Thinking Read Aloud. By asking "why" questions, you can help students process their thinking about information that may not be *right there* in the text but where they have to meld ideas together without the book stating it explicitly. These inferences occur spontaneously, as students might ask deeper questions, which are not answered in the text and are not surface-level questions. Inferences help the reader to elaborate on what they understand from text, therefore constructing new knowledge. Readers can form a mental representation that matches the text (Nirchi, 2014).

Multilingual students can be involved in complex interactions around text appropriate to their language acquisition level. Students do not only need to be involved in literal, or recall, questions; they can be involved in questioning that spurs the growth in reading comprehension strategies (Duke & Block, 2012). Teachers should be aware of the types of questions they ask students during instruction to ensure they are encouraging multilingual students to talk about their reading and practice oral language.

Conducting a Deep-Thinking Read Aloud

Step 1. When reading, the teacher wants to facilitate discussion so that the students are doing the thinking and the talking about the text. The first step in the strategy encourages students to think about what kinds of things they can say about text. When students go back and reflect on what was read, they process the information in the text in order to comprehend language and meaning (Cain & Oakhill, 1999).

In this step, the teacher also reads aloud to the students. Reading aloud and talking together encourages students to develop schema related to the topic of text. She discusses the types of statements that could be made during or after reading the text. A statement that we can back up with evidence is a claim.

A claim is a clear, concise statement about a topic or point that the speaker (writer) is making. When the teacher asks students to answer questions about what was read to them, she focuses on not just asking recall questions—also known as surface level questions. She asks the students to make a claim about what they think about the text. While she is presenting the minilesson, she creates an anchor chart that provides a visual for students about what a claim is and how they might go about making a claim.

Step 2. The second step in the process is when the teacher talks about her thinking to reveal her thinking for the students. This step is short, as the goal was not to give the students answers about what they should think about the text but to model how the thinking process is working. Thinking aloud helps students understand what is going on in the teacher's mind as she works through a text.

So to do this, the teacher reads a part of the text and then models deep thinking for students. She can discuss what deep thinking is with students (when we go beyond the surface of the text to answer a question). Then by thinking aloud, the teacher asks a question aloud that only she intends to answer. The teacher doesn't elicit responses from the students yet. The teacher asks herself a question that cannot be answered easily and then models how students can dive deep into the text to figure out the answer.

The teacher used "why" questions to model this step. "Why" questions work really well for modeling this task. For a deep dive into text, the teacher might need to model using language like this, "Here on page thirteen, the text says . . . [Quote]. I am wondering why the [character name] is . . . I am thinking this because . . ." This could also be a time for the teacher to model how she is making an inference.

Step 3. Step 3 is about the teacher beginning to release responsibility. Students learn and develop as readers when they participate (Kong & Fitch, 2002). Moving the focus of the discussion from the teacher modeling to the students thinking about text and talking about why they think what they do shifts ownership and responsibility for the learning to the learners for the conversation.

Now that the teacher has modeled deep thinking through the think aloud for students, she can set them up to ask deep questions about the text themselves. They can write the questions on sticky notes and share them with each other. Or they can work in pairs to ask the questions, recording them in a reading journal. The teacher can encourage students to then answer the questions they ask by making a statement and going back to the text to back up their statement. They will be doing what the teacher modeled in Step 2.

Together with students, the teacher adds to the anchor chart information, discussing *claim* and *evidence*. The teacher can facilitate a class-created definition of each term and record it. Then, using a book or text that he has already read with the students, he can write a few examples of a claim and the evidence that backs up the claim on the chart.

Here is an example:

- "In *The Flower* by John Light, Brigg's seeds did not grow, and he was very sad. Page 20 shows that he is sad because it says 'Brigg was very disappointed,' and he looked sad in the picture. When I wondered about how sad Brigg was, I went back and thought about how dreary his city was and how there were no flowers."

Step 4. In the fourth step, the teacher is giving students time to discuss their thinking. This not only helps them to solidify their thinking and check their comprehension, but it also creates an atmosphere in the classroom where the students have knowledge and authority as readers. The teacher can invite students to share their statements with the class, having the students think aloud with the class about what they said and why. They can also share the questions they asked themselves to get to the deeper thinking. Each student can share his or her statement and what phrase or sentence in the book supports the statement they wrote down.

> "Every learner discovers what they think, what they feel, and what still alludes them by talking."

Students may not spontaneously know how to respond to each other in discussion. So they can begin by just popping up and saying what they wrote on their sticky note; the sharing may go in succession, student by student. After students develop confidence in sharing their thinking, they might be able to comment on each other's thinking by using phrases like, "I was also thinking . . . ," or "I can add on to that idea with my own thought. . . ." You can model how to add on to another person's idea and chart conversation starters that can help students add on. Some sentence frames include the following:

- "I can add on to that."
- "I had a similar idea."
- "My idea is related."
- "I also noticed."

Looking Ahead

Every learner discovers what they think, what they feel, and what still alludes them by talking. Speaking and listening solidify understandings and skills, and develop social connections, which are so important for multilingual learners. So as you dip in and out of the chapters that follow, I encourage you to revisit this oral language development chapter for reminders.

CHAPTER SIX

Phonics and Spelling

There are thousand of reasons why this chapter was the toughest for me to write. Most have to do with the sheer scope of teaching phonics and spelling. The challenge was to decide on a particular lens that would be most helpful to you in teaching multilingual students. To do that well, I am focusing on the key skills and routines for small group settings and leaving the bigger background on teaching phonics in the capable hands of other authors, whose books I recommend on page 108. So my premise is this: Children who are multilingual learners and children who are deemed "below level" are getting overloaded with far too much phonics in isolation. To correct this, this chapter shares ideas for teaching phonics and spelling in the context of meaningful texts so that you develop students' alphabetic knowledge *along with* other important dimensions of becoming a reader—and being part of a community of readers.

COMMON CHALLENGES

Twenty years ago, Wiley Blevins (2010) made the point that phonics is a crucial but single step in a series of steps through the gateway and into the vast landscape of reading. Yet what happens is that schools invest in phonics and reading resources meant to catch up every child, and schools wind up using them haphazardly. A multilingual student gets phonics in small groups, whole group, in a resource room, with a speech and language pathologist, with a tutor, for homework. It's counterproductive and not effective for multilingual learners. They need to be developing fluency with letters and sounds, of course, but in tandem with experiences with books that help them develop fluency socially and academically. The only way to do that is to read and discuss texts alongside the phonics instruction and to make instruction dynamic (Blevins, 2020). In his book *Meaningful Phonics and Word Study*, Blevins states:

> For me, the best phonics instruction is active, engaging, and thought-provoking. Students are playing with letters and sounds, discussing what they observe about how words work to deepen their understanding of the alphabetic system to read. Phonics instruction involves talk. It involves observation. And it involves ongoing application, with lots of authentic reading and writing experiences to get mastery so that the skills can be transferred to all reading situations.

At the reading table, remember it's never about teaching phonics; it's always about teaching children to engage in reading.

Attributes of Dynamic Phonics Instruction

Play, talk, discover—instruction involves students learning actively. I would add that phonics instruction is dynamic because it reflects the changing makeup of students at the table, their diverse backgrounds, and their differing needs, as evident in these recommendations from the NSW Department of Education and Training Learning Development (2009). In italics, I've added brushstrokes of what it might look and sound like before and during a lesson.

- Establish what students already know about phonics. *Often during I-do modeling, use phrases like "I know you know the sound this letter makes!" and "Let's think about how to say this word; what letters do you see and what sounds to they make?"*

- Provide opportunities for students to demonstrate their phonics knowledge in different ways. *We do, You do; you might invite them to sound out a word while reading a text on their own or chunk a word into syllables and then sound out the syllables while reading a text. You can have them practice sounding out in isolation, but tie students' experiences to text and books as often as possible.*

- Plan for and differentiate phonics instruction to meet students' different learning needs. *For example, students new to English need to know the alphabet and the letter sounds, while students who are emerging readers in English need support in sounding out words while reading a text.*

- Group students responsively to accommodate the diverse range of phonics learning needs in the classroom, understanding that groupings will be flexible and change as students' needs change. *Organize students into groups based on what they are able to do with texts and with figuring out words. So if students are reading fairly easy books, group them together, and if students are able to read books with more complicated texts that have multisyllabic words, group them together. They don't have to be reading at the same level in leveled text; they just need to be working on the same skills in phonics. Often, these students might be at different stages of language acquisition. Perhaps some students are able to talk casually and get around the school well, where other students are still not as confident talking in English—but if they have the same needs in phonics, you can group them together.*

- Draw upon the rich and varied experiences and understandings that each student brings to the classroom. *Involve students in talking about their ideas and experiences and then write class messages, sounding out the words together, giving students the opportunities to write the sounds they hear. They might share ideas about their favorite foods that they eat at home or what they do with their families for special occasions.*

- Make connections between students' experiences and the learning of new phonics knowledge. *During We do and You do, habitually ask them about their own ideas, such as "What can you tell me is your favorite thing to do with your family? Let's write that down together." Bridge students' answers by restating their words in a way that bridges what they shared to the new learning about how to spell words.*

Dynamic phonics instruction actually goes beyond the borders of phonics and spelling, touching upon word work, vocabulary, comprehension, and writing. In this light, as you plan lessons, you can select activities from Chapters 5 through 9, as they all address teaching children to read. This chapter and Chapter 8 on Word Work most directly cover early reading. Kilpatrick (2015) identified three levels in learning to read:

> Level 1: *Phonics.* Children learn letter names and the sounds of the letters.

> Level 2: *Decoding.* Children combine letter–sound knowledge with phonological blending to sound out new words (word identification).

> Level 3: *Orthographic mapping.* Children efficiently expand their sight vocabularies (word recognition).

Phonics and Spelling Resources

Meaningful Phonics and Word Study by Wiley Blevins

A Fresh Look at Phonics by Wiley Blevins

Partner Poems & Word Ladders by Harrison, Rasinski, and Fresch

Begin With Phonemic Awareness

Initially, multilingual students will need to work on hearing the sounds in English. Therefore, it is important to teach phonemic awareness. Phonemic awareness is the awareness that words are made up of a series of discrete phonemes, or sounds. Phonemes are the smallest units of language. Phonemic awareness focuses on spoken language, whereas phonics involves the relationships between sounds and written letters or spellings (Snider, 1995; Blevins, 2017).

Immersion in Spoken Sounds

Multilingual students need to be immersed in the sounds of the English language. With students at the **beginning** and

emerging levels of proficiency, use entertaining poetry, songs, rhymes, and chants for your shared text (see Phonics and Spelling Resources box on page 108 for some good sources for these materials). For young students, you can sing and say nursery rhymes; you can sing students' songs and recite poetry. For older students, you can recite poetry and expose students to poetry and prose that plays with language.

Following are several types of activities that progress from easy to more complex.

Rhyme and alliteration: Start simple, with activities that teach rhyme and alliteration. Some include the following:

- Help students identify the rhyming and nonrhyming sounds while you are working with the text.

- When you sense they are ready, invite them to come up with some rhyming words.

- Together, enjoy alliteration, with sentences like Mother Goose's "Three grey geese in a green field grazing." Ask students, "Can you identify the repeated sound?"

- To practice noticing assonance, say aloud a sentence containing words that mostly have the same vowel sound, as in "The brown bear at the fair ate the pear and did not care."

Sound categorizing: To sort sounds, students can work with real objects or pictures that **start with an initial consonant sound.** For example, show a picture of a cat for the sound /k/ or a picture of a dog for the sound /d/. You would ask students what they see in the pictures. Honor them for how they answer. Students might answer in their heritage language. You can then ask them the sounds they hear in the word in their heritage language (such as /p/ for *perro*- meaning *dog*). Then, discuss the name of the object on the card in English and share the sound at the beginning of the word. Say it slowly and talk with students about how to say the sounds either in their heritage language or in English.

The cards can be of pictures that represent **long** or **short vowels** but should not be blended sounds. It is best to have a few pictures of each sound so students can practice hearing an initial consonant sound with more than one word/object. Students can practice the sounds in groups—for example, they might have cards with pictures of a cat, cake, and carrot for /k/.

Present a few cards at a time at first for students to work on recognizing the sound.

 Visit the companion website for sample sound cards.

Sound sorting: Next, work on *sorting* the sounds by combining a few cards together that represent different sounds and have the students sort the sounds into groups. This gives them practice in noticing important and common sound/spelling patterns. For example, a sorting group could include *cake, dog, bake, carrot, king, doctor, bicycle, book.* Work in groups up to 18 pictures that represent three to four phonemes (Walpole & McKenna, 2007).

To categorize sounds, you invite students to practice in three ways: pictures of objects that have a similar beginning, middle, or ending sound. For instance, you can provide the following three pictures and have students categorize which go together: *coat, goat, goal* or *mag, mug, sun.*

To ask students to match the ending sound, say, "Which two words end with the same sound?" Students would identify which word/picture does not match the group based on the sound (Snider, 1995). Provide practice for students to categorize sounds varying between initial, medial, and final sounds.

Examples of prompts for sorting include the following:

Rhyme: Which word does not rhyme?

Initial consonant: Which two words begin with the same sound?

Medial sounds (long vowels): Which two words do not have the same middle sound?

Medial sounds (short vowels): Which two words have the same middle sound?

Medial sounds (consonants, as in words like *mitten* or *stirring*): Which two words have the same middle sound?)

Refresher

Phonemic awareness terms give most of us flashbacks to preservice classes! Here is a refresher for you, along with kid-friendly ways to say them to students.

Rime: the vowel and everything after the syllable	Look at this part of a word (-in). Let's say it together; I know you know it!
Onset: the consonant, consonant blend, or consonant diagraph that precedes the rime in the syllable	Check out what happens when I put a consonant in front of the rime (the part of the word I just showed you); what does it say now?
Phoneme: sound	Ooohhh, words have lots of sounds in them. We call these phonemes. Let's practice saying sounds we hear in words!
Initial = beginning, medial = middle, final = ending	The sounds at the beginning are the initial sounds. Listen to this word, "cake." What is the initial sound (phoneme)? What sound do you hear in the middle (the medial sound)? What sound do you hear at the end of the word (final phoneme)?

Blending

In this kind of word building, you ask students to make a word, such as *sat.* The primary goal is for them to blend, or sound out, the word.

Focus first on blending and make it fun and game-like! Model the sound in the words, saying them slowly or elongating them as needed. Then, say the sounds fast. Say the words slow for students and then have them say the sounds fast, blending to make the word, mmmmmmm/aaaaaa/nnnnnn, man, p/aaaaaa/t, pat.

Segmenting

When teaching students to segment sounds, you reverse the sequence that you did with blending. You say the word, and then the students say the sounds they hear in the word slowly. For example, say *man,* and the students would say mmmmm/aaaaa/nnnn, and then say it without stretching the sounds, /m/ /a/ /n/. You can begin with two-phoneme words and then move on to three-phoneme words and also four-phoneme words. Four-phoneme words will most likely have consonant blends in them, so they are more difficult (Walphole & McKenna, 2007). Remember that you are focusing on the sounds, not the spelling of the words, so this is just an oral activity.

Say It, Move It

This activity is a bit more complex than just blending and segmenting sounds. You will need manipulatives to do these activities—cubes, buttons, or pennies work well. You can progress through levels of complexity by beginning with syllables, working with onset and rimes, and then individual phoneme sounds.

For additional scaffolding, provide students with Elkonin boxes (see appendix on page 206 for student mats with different Elkonin boxes), as it makes it easier for them to visualize the word. Have students move the manipulative (the penny or cube) into the box as they say the syllable, onset-rime, or phoneme.

The mat matches the correct number of Elkonin boxes based on the number of syllables or phonemes in the words you are working with. For example, onset and rimes use a mat with two boxes (one box for the onset sound and one box for the rime). You can begin with two-phoneme words and then move on to three-phoneme words and four-phoneme words. Four-phoneme words will most likely have consonant blends in them so they are more difficult (Walphole & McKenna, 2007).

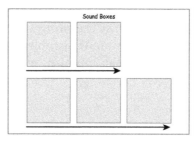 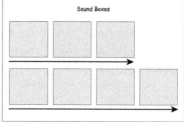

Don't Overdo It

It is important to teach blending and segmenting as part of phonemic awareness and phonics instruction, but don't overdo it. Students who are exposed to intensive phoneme manipulation programs and who are not developmentally ready for it may be discouraged as learners (Bowey, 2002). For multilingual learners, it helps to do the work in the context of the book you are reading. For example, have students work with words that are in the book ahead of reading the book. Then the reading of the book provides meaningful practice.

Deleting and Adding Phonemes to Make New Words.

The next step would be to work with students to make a new word by deleting sounds from a word or add a sound to a phoneme to make a word. (For example, change *sat* to *mat*.) This is cognitively more demanding than the blending-focused word building (Blevins, 2017), so it's important to present the activity as a game of playing with sounds, language play—use a fun, light tone. You can begin with onset and rimes and then move to three- and four-phoneme words.

You would start with modeling (always model first!). To focus on onset and rime, say a word based on a rime—for instance, *man.* Say, "take the /m/ away and what sounds are left? *an.* Or say a three-phoneme word, *cake*, and segment the word, /k/, /a/, /k/ and say, "take away the /k/ and what is left?"

Once you work on deleting sounds, you can work on adding sounds. It works well to start with onset and rimes. Start with the rime *ip.* Then prompt the students to add a sound. Say, "Add /p/ to *ip.*" The students would respond *pip.*

Substituting and Reversing

Substituting and reversing is another skill in phonemic awareness that students need to practice. Since this is phonemic awareness, the sound games you are playing are all oral games; you do not need to work with letters. In substituting sounds, you would prompt students to change a sound in a word with another sound. You can start with onset and rimes and work up to three- and four-phoneme words that are not necessarily onset and rimes. You would model first and then prompt the students. You would say, "Change the /m/ in *map* to /s/. What is the word? Say _____. Say _____" The students would say *map,* then *sap.*

Working with reversing sounds in words is also helpful for students in learning to manipulate sounds. You would say a word and prompt students to say the sounds in reverse. You would say, "Say _____. Say the sounds in _____. Now, say the sounds backward _____." The students would respond. For example, if you said *ram,* students would say *ram,* /r/ /a/ /m/, then /m/ /a/ /r/.

"For multilingual learners, it helps to do the work in the context of the book you are reading."

Phonemic Awareness Teaching Examples

Phoneme isolation	What is the first sound in these words? What is the last sound in these words?	Pickle, pot, paste Leaf, giraffe, golf
Phoneme identification, counting, and categorization	Count the sounds in this word. What sounds do not belong?	Past, map, knife Goat, moat, got
Phoneme blending	Blend the sounds to make a word.	/m/ /i/ /i/ /c/ /l/ /a/ /p/
Phoneme segmenting	Say the sounds in this word.	Man, boy mist
Phoneme deletion	Say _____. Say _____ without the _____.	Cake /c/ ake Rap /r/ ap
Phoneme addition	Add _____ to _____. What word would you have?	/s/ flow, flows /cl/ over, clover
Phoneme substitution	Say _____. Change _____ to _____.	Map /m/ /s/ sap
Phoneme reversal	Say the sounds in _____. Now say the sounds backward.	Tisk, /t/ /i/ /sk/ /sk/ /i/ /t/

Adapted from Kindervaten (2012).

You can work on phonemic awareness while working on phonics skills (coming in the next section). While students need a strong foundation in hearing sounds in words, we don't teach the skills in a linear fashion by doing phonemic awareness first and then phonics. We weave them together. Depending on how many authentic and engaging literacy experiences you provide in your classroom and engage multilingual learners with, generally, within one school year, most students at the **entering** and **emerging** levels will be able to hear and manipulate sounds in words; at the **bridging** level, phonemic awareness work reaches into helping students move to phonics and encoding words so that they can spell mostly accurately and communicate well in writing. Students at the **bridging** levels would also have fun making up new words, rhyming, and playing with language. Students at the **reaching** level would generally not need phonemic awareness instruction because phonemic awareness is an early skill and oral, but you can combine it with phonics instruction at the reading table to reflect learners' readiness to play with language, write, and spell by using the sounds they hear in words.

PHONICS

Phonics is the connection between sounds, letters, and combinations of letters. As students build the ability to hear the sounds, then they can work on writing down or pointing out the corresponding letters (Birsh & Birsh, 2018). Start the phonics work by focusing on words that students are already familiar with and present the words in context (Gibbons, 2015). In other words, use general vocabulary that students understand when you say the words; they don't have to know how to read the words.

Teaching sounds without connecting to some sort of meaningful context will not help students acquiring English connect to the points you are teaching. For instance, if you teach how to sound out a word, start with words that would be more familiar to students so that when they learn to read it and later write it, they can use it purposefully. These might be words that they use to talk and share ideas with each other; avoid lots of academic vocabulary at this point.

Decoding

As I said earlier, the goal of phonics is to help students decode words. How? Because phonics helps students learn how to map sounds onto letters and spellings of words; the more children can do this efficiently, the more they can decode. The more they can decode, the more they can comprehend! Decoding is the ability to combine letter–sound knowledge with phonological blending to sound out new words. That's a formal way of talking about word recognition skills. When we talk about decoding, we often talk about how it puts students on track to reading fluently. In reading fluently, they don't have to focus on figuring out the words, and instead, they can think about what the words mean.

The challenge for multilingual students. English learners may build their abilities to decode words but still have no idea what the words mean that they are decoding. It is for this reason that the lesson sequences (see Chapter 4) include lots of vocabulary and oral language development. We also support decoding by using texts containing enough decodable words when we determine what our students need at an early stage of phonics instruction. Using controlled, decodable texts at the beginning levels of reading instruction helps students develop a sense of comfort in—and control over—their reading growth. The tight connection between what students learn in phonics and what they read is essential for building a foundation faster in early reading. This foundation is especially important when students encounter less-controlled leveled readers at the reading table. These decodable texts can be a tool in your toolbox used briefly, as needed, but they can also be supportive to **entering** and **emerging** level readers.

Letter-Name and Letter–Sound Associations

When you start teaching sounds, you will first make sure that students know letter-name and letter–sound associations. Students who are young readers learn the letter—or to them the squiggly lines—that represent each letter. If a student is older and learning English and comes from a language background that does not use the Roman alphabet, they will need time to play with the English alphabet. While they will know the alphabet and sounds in their primary language, they will need to know the alphabet—how the lines form English letters and sounds (Walpole & McKenna, 2007).

In some languages, the letter–sound connection is 1:1. For every sound there is a letter (Gooch & Lambirth, 2008). English learners will have to learn that this is not the case for English. There is not a 1:1 correspondence between sounds and letters in English. For example, diagraphs are two letters that make one sound, *ea.* Students need to learn that when they see the letters in diagraphs together, they don't pronounce them separately, as they might in their primary language, but that the combination of letters has its own sound. There are 44 sounds but only 26 letters in English. Students will also need to learn that one letter can make more than one sound; notice the different sounds *a* makes in *cat, car, make,* and *talk* (Gooch & Lambirth, 2008). A sequence in which you can introduce the letters to maximize being able to make words is a m t s i f d r o g l h u c b n k v e w j p y x q z. Find a list of recommended letters and sounds to teach in the appendix. The following table provides information on phonics instructional goals.

Phonics Instructional Goals

Letter names	Introduce in an order to maximize making words a m t s i f d r o g l h u c b n k v e w j p y x q z
Consonant sounds	Introduce in an order to maximize making words m t s f d r g l h c b n k v w j p x q z
Consonant blends	bl, cl, fl, gl, pl, sl, br, cr, dr, fr, gr, pr, tr, sc, sk, sm, sn, sp, st, sw, tw, scr, shr, spl, spr, str, thr
Diagraphs & tigraphs	Ch, sh, ng, ph, th, wh, tch, dge
Vowel sounds	Short and long sounds represented by a single letter
Long vowel sounds with alternative spelling	ai, ay, a-e maid, play, made ee, ea, e-e, ei, y bee, beneath, hungry ie, igh, y, i-e pie, light, my, pike ow, oe, o-e slow, toe, dote u-e use
Short vowel sounds with alternative spelling	e, ea bed, deadi i, y tip, myth u, o mud, come, mother

(Continued)

(Continued)

Dipthongs	oi, oy	oil, boy
	ou, ow	out, how
	eu, ew	eureka, few
	ure	sure
	ai	pair
R-controlled vowels	ar, er, ir, or, ur	
Orthographic similarity, intrasyllable linguistic rime	-an, -ap, -at, -aw,- ay, -in, -ip, -it, -op, -ot, -ug, -ack, -ail-, -ain, -ake, -ale, -all, -ame, -amp, -ank, -ash, -ate, -eat, -ell, -est, -ice, -ick, -ide, -ill, -ine, -ing, -ink-, -ock, -oke, -old, -ore, -uck, -ump, -unk, -ight	
Morphemes	Prefixes, suffixes	

Adapted from Bald, 2007; Tolman, 2005; Westwood, 2001.

Decoding: Letters-Sounds-Blending

Students are taught in very short, quick activities small groups of letter sounds that they can then blend together (NSW, 2022). Students are shown the letters, the teacher prompts them to say the sounds the letters represent, and the students blend the sounds to read the word: *pot, stop, pot*. See the preceding figure for a sequence of introducing letters. You can teach known letter–sound combinations to teach CV and CVC words: *at, cat*. When working with students, blend phonemes in order through all of the word to read the word. Students can also build the word with magnetic letters or write the word on small whiteboards. Segment a word into its phonemes to spell the word, /c/-/a/-/t/, **cat**. Teach words that are regular; you will teach frequently occurring irregular words as sight words. Move on to teaching CCVC words and CVCC words.

> You can introduce the letters in a m t s i f d r o g l h u c b n k v e w j p y x q z. Vowels are taught separately.

TEACH IT!

WORD BUILDING

1. Model the new word using magnetic letters, letter cards, or writing on a whiteboard. Say: "I can read the word by saying the sound for each letter and then blending the sounds together."

2. Point to each letter and say the sound: /c/ /a/ /t/.

3. Put a finger over/under letters and model blending the word: *cat.*

4. Model how to build or write the word. "If I pull the sounds apart, I can write the word _____ by putting the letters together." Model pulling the word apart and building the word.

5. Give students a new word, preferably a word that appears in the text they will read. Provide the letters for the word. "Build the word *man* using your sounds."

6. Provide support as students build the word.

7. Say, "Now say each sound in the word." After students say each sound, say "Now blend the sounds together to read the word." Provide support for students as they blend.

Print-Sound Code

When students learn that each sound is represented by a grapheme, or group of graphemes, they are breaking what is known and the print-sound code. Students need to work on *encoding* words while they are learning to *decode* words. Use small whiteboards and markers to practice writing words. Tell them that they are going to write using a vowel, *a,* and remind them what sound it makes /a/. Say the word you are teaching the students to spell: *cat.* Clap the number of sounds in the word cat; have students clap the words. Model: "the first sound is /c/"; write a *c* on your whiteboard. The next sound is

/a/; write an *a* on your whiteboard. The next sound is /t/; write a *t* on your whiteboard. Then ask students to help you say the word. After you model once, give students time to write words on their whiteboards following the same pattern. Begin with CV words, and as students gain ability, move to CVC words, CVCC words, and CCVC words.

TEACH IT!

WORD BUILDING

1. Say the word you want to teach students to write. Clap the sounds in the word.

2. Model writing the first sound, the next sound, and the last sound.

3. Ask students to help you read the word.

4. Now it's the students turn. Say a new word. Ask students to clap the sounds in the word.

5. Students say the sound in the word and write the corresponding letter down on their whiteboard.

6. Ask students to read the word they wrote.

ANALOGY

When students learn to recognize words through analogy, they are recognizing how the spelling of an unknown word is similar to a known word (Ehri & McCormick, 1998). When analogizing, students recognize the spelling pattern and then adjust pronunciation to work with the new word. An example of this is *train, main*. If students recognize the spelling pattern *ain*, then they can learn to manipulate the first sound and substitute /m/ for the blend /tr/. When we work with students with what is called onset and rime, we are teaching analogy phonics. When students have been exposed to onsets and rimes, they will be able to use the rimes to read words, and most students who can read at the preprimer level have onset and rime knowledge (Bowey, 2002; Goswami & Mead, 1992).

Common rimes have similar spelling sequences: *man, pan, can*. The onset in this example is a single phoneme: /m/, /p/, /c/. You can teach onset and rimes to students learning English after teaching some phoneme manipulation— you want students to understand that the first sound is a phoneme and can be manipulated or changed. In *man, pan, can*, the first sound in *man*, /m/, is changed for /p/. Teach onsets and rimes by first showing students the rime, for example *an*, and then work with the students to change out the first sound. To teach this, you might show the rime on a whiteboard or with magnetic letters and say, "Say *an*." You would add a *p* and then say, "Add /p/ to *an*; now what does it say /p/, /a/, /n/?" You go through the list manipulating the first sound. A list of onset and rimes is available to download from the companion website .

TEACH IT!

ONSET RIME

1. Show the rime.

2. Model saying the rime and tell students: "Say the rime _____." Point to the rime while the students say the rime.

3. Add a single letter as the onset. Say the sound and point to the letter and prompt the students to say it.

4. Read the word all together, running your finger under the word to indicate that the students need to blend the onset and rime together.

SIGHT WORDS

Sight words are words that are stored in memory and are read as a unit automatically (Ehri, 2005). The terms "sight words" and "high-frequency words" are often used synonymously to describe words that fluent readers can read automatically. However, there is an important distinction to make here; high-frequency words are those that are most commonly used in English, while sight words are those that we can read without decoding each letter–sound combination in the word. As fluent readers, most of the words we read are sight words, and all of them are high-frequency words. When students have a large bank of sight words, they spend less cognitive effort decoding words and can spend more cognitive effort on comprehension (LaBerge & Samuels, 1974). Sight word knowledge is also helpful because students will learn the meaning of the words and connect meaning

(Continued)

(Continued)

to the word automatically (Ehri & McCormick, 1998). Flash card intervention has been shown to be successful in helping students learning to read with automaticity, and therefore, they can focus more on comprehension of the text they are reading (January et al., 2017). Traditional drill of sight words with flashcards has shown to be successful when teaching students sight words (Burns & Sterling-Turner, 2010).

Traditional drill only takes place for a few minutes of the time at the reading table, and it is easy to prep. Drill isn't a bad thing if it is used in small doses for a specific skill and then you move on. Drill isn't a good thing if it takes over the time you should be spending working with students in relevant text that engages them as readers, so keep this instruction short.

Traditional drill of sight words occurs *after* the student has been taught the sounds in the word and to decode the word by sound. Once you have done this orthographic mapping, move to traditional drill. In traditional drill, the new word is modeled. You say, "This word is _____." And then you prompt the students, "Say _____." Once the words in the current stack are presented initially, you show the words and ask students to say the word, giving them corrective feedback in order to say the word correctly. Once you go through the stack, you will want to shuffle the words so that you are not presenting them in the same order (January et al., 2017). This is very quick, as you have other activities to accomplish during small group reading instruction. Keep the stack of words short each day in order to ensure that you don't spend too much time on any given day on sight words. You can add in new sight words once students can say the word when they see it. It is also a good idea to add sight words that have been mastered into the stack periodically to ensure students maintain their knowledge of the sight word. A sight word list adapted from Fry's sight word list appears in the companion website. This list includes 100 words, and you should focus on words in each segment before moving onto words on the next list.

TEACH IT!

SIGHT WORDS

Show and model the new word. "This word is _____."

Prompt the students, "Say _____."

Go through the current stack of words using Steps 1 and 2. Once they have introduced the words, go through the stack prompting, "Say the word."

Shuffle the words so that you are not presenting them in the same order and go through the stack, prompting for the word. "Say the word."

Early Writing and Spelling

iStock.com/Sushiman

Writing involves more than spelling, but it helps to focus on students' spelling development to understand how they are developing language skills in order to express themselves. Very young students or early spellers learn to write words that represent their thoughts by relying simply on the sounds they hear. For example, an early speller might write the letter *B* for the word *bee* (Treiman, & Treiman, 2015). As students develop an understanding of the phoneme (sound) and grapheme (written letter) relationships, they will match sounds to letters as they write (Gentry, 1982). For example, students will begin to segment the phonemes /k/, /ae/, /t/ with the graphemes 'c', 'a', 't' (Varnhagen et al., 1997). As students develop in literacy, they become aware of the inconsistencies of the letter to sound correspondences in English (the same sound can be spelled different ways, *ea* in *seat* but *ee* in *seek)* and develop understanding of how words are spelled based on syntax, semantics, and phonology. As they continue to grow, they learn about the morphology of words and how words are put together—for example, how prefixes and suffixes can be added to root words.

Five Stages of Spelling Development

Generally, there are five stages of spelling development, represented in the graphic that follows. Our instruction with phonemic awareness, phonics, and writing helps move students through the stages. We can encourage the sound-out strategy to help students learn to spell words to get their thoughts on paper when teaching writing at the reading table. Because the small group instruction during reading should be focused on *reading,* writing at the table with you would be discontinued and students will write about their reading away from the table, independently, once they become close to correct spellers.

Transitional spellers can certainly write independently, but as their phonics instruction continues, you can have them write at the table with you to practice their sound–spelling work. As they develop to transitional spellers, you can encourage them to use what they know about how words work to spell words. For instance, if you have been working with onset and rimes, they may know and remember how to spell certain words based on the rime: *cake, lake, bake.* Also, as students work on phonics they will learn the different ways that the sound long /e/ can be spelled and in what contexts certain spellings are used: e, ee, ea, _e_e, ey, ie, ei, _____y.

Developmental Stages in Students' Spelling

Stage	Example	Knowledge/Strategies
Precommunicative	૧	Symbols represent
Semiphonetic	IL	Alphabetic strategy; beginning to sound out words
Phonetic	Lil	Sounding out words
Transitional	Litl	Partial correct spelling; beginning to see how letters combine to make sounds
Correct	Little	Complete phonological understanding; using spelling conventions and rules; morphological connections to form words

Adapted from Varnhagen et al. (1997).

Assessment of Spelling Levels

While understanding the stages of spelling development is helpful in designing instruction, there is more to consider. Students' literacy experiences in their primary language influences their development in being able to write in English (Bear & Smith, 2012). Students' ability to learn to write and spell is influenced by students' understanding about words, sounds, and spelling patterns (Treiman & Kessler, 2014). Knowing that students learn to write words through understanding context links to language, morphology, and how print works in English can help us provide instruction to English learners.

Students acquiring English may get the context wrong at first—for example, they might want to write *past* /pæst/ but instead write *passed*. Learning which word is correct and which word works correctly within sentences takes time for multilingual learners. What helps students learn these differences is lots of experiences with texts, reading, and playing with language. Students will learn how to spell words based on their knowledge about how words look and also by using phonological understanding and the phonemes (sounds) around it. It is the context of the use of the word that influences the choice (Treiman, 2017).

There are general guidelines of spelling development that can help you determine next steps for instruction. You can give students a list of words to spell and then note their development level and correspond what you are seeing in their spelling with the level and then act based on what the students know and what the next step would be. Take a look at the spelling development in the following table. The developmental spelling stages are described in five sections: precommunicative, prephonetic, phonetic, transitional—which includes patterns within-words and syllable juncture—and derivational meaning (Bear, 2007; Invernizzi & Hayes, 2004; Varnhagen et al., 1997). You can note what students are able to do in the spelling assessment and help them move to the next step through instruction.

Spelling Development

Precommunicative	Prephonetic	Phonetic	Transitional		Derivational Meaning	Correct Spelling
			Patterns within words	Syllable juncture		
	B for bee	/k/ /æ/ /t/ c-a-t	shep for ship trane for train	confedent opasishion	confedent opasishion	confident opposition
Child makes random marks	Alphabetic or letter-name strategy; where the letter represents the sounds	Consistently sounds out words and matches phoneme to grapheme; can break word into phonemes and match each phoneme with a letter	Spells words with orthographic similarity; spells common orthographic units correctly (rimes); spells correctly most single-syllable short vowel words correctly; spells consonant blends; spells diagraphs	Uses cues to spell based on how words break into syllables; uses orthographic connections	Aware of roots and affixes; uses morphological based spelling strategies; understands internal structure of words	

By giving a student a list of words to spell, you can match what the student is doing in their spelling to the chart and then decide on a course of action.

Mercedes is a second-grade speller. We can see her spelling assessment in the image below. Mercedes appears to be a within-word pattern speller based on the spelling development continuum. The next teaching step would be to continue working with Mercedes on hearing the sounds within words and understanding how to represent those sounds in words, using both the phonology of the word and the semantics and syntax of the word in sentences (deciding if the correct word is *past* or *passed,* as they both sound the same but have different semantic meanings. See the appendix for suggested word lists for spelling assessments.

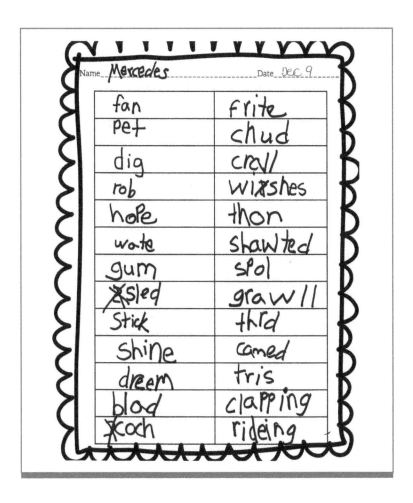

Looking Ahead

Remember that multilingual learners need time to play with language, think about the sounds they hear in words, what sounds letters make as they decode *while* reading text, and how to spell and express themselves effectively in writing.

CHAPTER SEVEN

Vocabulary

iStock.com/SeventyFour

When I am working with teachers, they often ask me, "How do I best help students learning to read while learning English?" They sometimes will implore; please tell me what to do because I feel like I'm not doing right by them. The concern and anxiety are understandable. We want them to grow as readers as quickly as possible, but the sheer amount of language they need to become good readers in English (and speakers of English too) is overwhelming. I know it is hard to meet all your students' needs on any given day. Actively teaching vocabulary will go a long way!

COMMON CHALLENGES

When it comes to expanding vocabulary in multilingual students, the most prevalent challenge I come across is this paradox: On the one hand, teachers put undue pressure on themselves and feel overwhelmed by the sheer amount of language multilingual students need to learn to become good readers in English. On the other hand, they sometimes presume that students will just "pick up" words in English if they are exposed to enough text with supportive pictures and visuals. Although it is true that students learn many words from reading widely and extensively (Feng & Webb, 2019), they also need direct instruction in vocabulary to increase their working and academic vocabularies. *They need both.* Keep this fact in mind, and you can rest assured that your vocabulary instruction for multilingual learners is sound.

Attributes of Dynamic Vocabulary Instruction

At the reading table, multilingual students get both direct instruction *and* the reading experiences that expose them to words. Dynamic vocabulary instruction bolsters students' motivation and word attack skills so that they have what they need to want to keep reading—during the school day and at home. Reading increases students' vocabularies faster than direct instruction. The more students read, the faster their vocabularies will increase (Duff et al., 2015).

Teaching vocabulary and expanding it for multilingual learners is about integration, meaningful use, and repetition. First, an overview of integration, which is not about teaching words in isolation but integrating them. It is about teaching words *in the context of texts*—the books you are reading together and those that students are reading on their own. By extension, you teach the words *in the context of meaningful conversation.* (Yes, you guessed it! Oral language development is coming into play.) When multilingual learners hear their teacher and peers using the new word in meaningful conversation about the story in their hands, it helps them remember it. And when you write the word on a chart or whiteboards during the lesson and invite them to write, you provide them with the all-important brain activation (see graphic on page 131).

Vocabulary instruction is also about repetition. Students need multiple opportunities to work with new words so that they can begin to own the words for themselves. Throughout this chapter, I provide activities that will help you provide this repetition.

And last but certainly not least, vocabulary instruction is about meaningful use. It's almost easier to define meaningful use by what it is not: It's not handing kids vocabulary lists and definitions and having them memorize it all for a quiz.

Meaningful use at the reading table means the new words are in the text or are a natural extension of the text. It means you as the teacher purposefully model using the word as you discuss the text with children and both repeat and slightly vary the ways you use the word as you discuss information, ideas, and personal connections to the text.

In the three sections that follow, we'll do a deeper dive into these three elements: integration, repetition, and meaningful use.

Integration

For students to really learn new words, the words need to connect existing knowledge to the new knowledge they are developing (Kersten, 2010; Nagy, 1988; Shin & Crandall, 2013; Rasinski et al., 2011). This is known as *integration*. By integrating word learning with known information, we help students as they create connections in their brains. But it's a particular set of connections that helps us *retain* the meaning of the words. According to brain research, three parts of the brain must be activated for us to learn a new word. These parts include where the sounds are stored, where the word's meaning is stored, and where the word's spelling (individual letters) is stored.

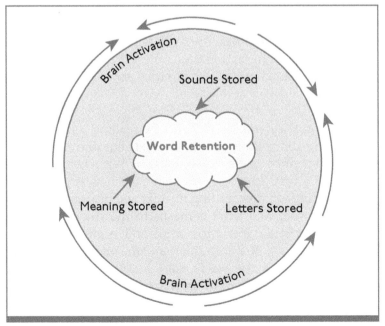

This brain research has implications for reading instruction; for spelling and word awareness work, the Read-Spell-Write-Extend Routine (Blevins, 2017) I shared in lesson sequences in Chapter 4 is an important one. In the context of vocabulary instruction, the principle is the same: We do routines that engage all parts of the brain needed to learn the word. For multilingual learners, we emphasize meaning, especially at the outset, because they sometimes don't yet have the conceptual understanding of the word that English-first students may have.

We guide this integration work primarily during small group conversations. In essence, we help the students create new schema. We can teach the word concepts (I discuss this more later). We can connect the words in text that are new to discussions we are having at the table—and use the words in the I-do (model) phase. You can have students practice the new words during collaborative work, through discussions and collaborative writing, and also in the You-do (independent practice) phase, when students are doing vocabulary activities or writing new sentences containing the words.

Repetition

Vocabulary instruction needs to include the repetition of new words (Blachowicz & Fisher, 2002; Ellis & Shintani, 2013; Nagy, 1988; Shin & Crandall, 2013; Stahl, 2004). At the reading table, you should be discussing words often, immersing students in new vocabulary words so that multilingual learners increase their vocabularies while working on their reading abilities. Students will not learn words by looking up words in dictionaries, unless the dictionary activities are embedded in reading and they are looking up words in context.

By contrast, they *will* learn words by reading lots of words and talking about the words in context. But don't just mention a word once and be done with it. With each repeated reading of a text, stop and talk about the new words, either before, during, or after reading the text and discuss the meaning of the word and what it means to the students so that they build schema about the word and begin to own the new words (Horst, 2010). In this way, students develop word-consciousness and the words start becoming part of their working vocabularies (Graves & Watts-Taffe, 2002).

Two pages from a "Guess the Word" vocabulary book

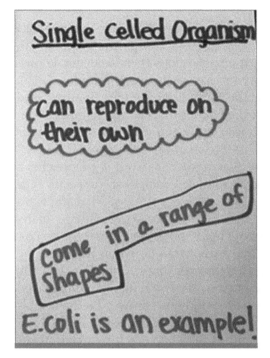
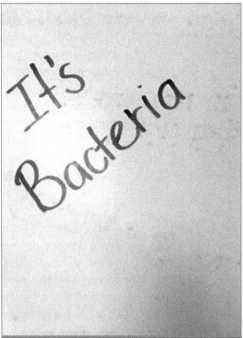

You can draw pictures about the words or create semantic maps. Nonlinguistic representations (this means ways of showing what words mean without using more words to indicate the meaning) of words can include acting out words, drawing word maps, categorizing words, and using lots of pictures and videos from the internet. Using nonlinguistic representations of words is a known way of helping students participate in meaningful repetition of new words (Marzano et al., 2001).

Meaningful Use

Students acquiring English grow their vocabularies faster when the words are embedded in meaningful contexts and they are given lots of opportunities to use the words over and over (Goldenburg, 2010). When students are involved in learning new words, the activities they are involved in need to be meaningful. Looking up words in a dictionary, unless directly connected to figuring out meaning in a text that students are reading, is **not** a meaningful way to learn words. This chapter provides multiple meaningful activities you can engage students in before, during, and after reading instruction at the reading table.

Begin With Teaching Word Concepts

When we teach vocabulary, we are teaching the concepts that words represent. This not only helps multilingual students learn the words, it also develops their academic knowledge and the vocabulary that connects to it (Cummins, 2010). Conceptual learning is the learning of the idea that the word identifies. In essence, words are just labels that represent concepts, and what we are teaching when we teach vocabulary is the concept plus the label. So when we teach a word, we need to teach the concept of that word. The word *dog* represents a specific type of four-legged animal. A *dalmatian* is a specific type of *dog*. The word itself carries the meaning of what the word represents. This is the trick to teaching vocabulary; so many times we focus on teaching *words,* but we need to focus on *concepts.* Words connect by concept too. So when teaching one word, we can often teach the words that connect conceptually to one specific word (Cameron, 2001). Think of antonyms and synonyms. Antonyms and synonyms connect the base word as either examples or nonexamples of the word. They have similar or opposite meanings. So when teaching words, focus on the **meaning.**

How do the language proficiency levels come into play?
Multilingual learners grow in their vocabulary development as they move through the language proficiency levels. However, becoming more fluent in English, often seen as the students' ability to speak English, doesn't always consider the acquisition of academic language. Students can acquire knowledge about the world in any language. This knowledge is just part of the students' knowledge bank (Cummins, 1981). When we teach concepts, we are teaching knowledge about the world and preparing multilingual students to read increasingly academic text.

What is academic language? Academic language is the language of content area texts. Informational texts (even for emergent readers) are filled with academic vocabulary about content areas—for example, books about bears or pets. Informational texts should be used at the reading table and used frequently (Duke et al., 2011; SEAL, 2021) for all grade levels. As students move from primary to upper grades, they will encounter academic vocabulary that is difficult.

What is the biggest challenge for multilingual learners? Textbooks and high-interest books have enough academic vocabulary in them that the comprehension of multilingual students can be severely compromised. Another problem is that textbooks and some high-interest books don't repeat the academic vocabulary or information; they have it appear only once or maybe twice. Multilingual students need what is called vocabulary recycling (Chacón-Beltrán et al., 2010) where words are seen and used multiple times. If it doesn't appear in text this way, then we need to provide opportunities to discuss the words and work with the words.

AN EXAMPLE WITH A TYPICAL TEXT

Let's take a deeper look at the idea that if students don't understand the vocabulary in a book, they won't comprehend what they are reading. Not only will they not comprehend the text, but the text also won't make sense. Consider the following text that comes from a second-grade leveled text about medicine.

> At that time, many people got sick from smallpox.
> This disease, or sickness, caused a high fever and
> pain. It also caused red spots all over the body.
> People sometimes died from smallpox.

Reprinted with permission of Benchmark Education from the book *Jenner & Fleming: Two Heroes of Medicine* by Laura Strom.

In this text, which words do you think would cause an English language learner who is about at the **developing** level in his language acquisition and who is an early reader a problem? It would most likely be *disease, sickness*, and *smallpox*. These are all the words that are *content*-related in this informational text. To make things worse, if we rely on the fix-up strategy of skipping words that students don't know, the student won't attempt to try to figure out the words' meaning (remember to say the words they need to be decoding, see Chapter 6) by using sentence clues or word parts and may just read to the end of the text, without any idea what the text is about. Also, if students try to figure out the word using the context of the paragraph but there are other words in the paragraph giving the student problems, she may still not understand the text.

Academic words become even more problematic for students as they move into upper grades. A fifth-grade book that could be used at the reading table is *Remarkable Roads*.

This book is about building roads, and it is filled with a large number of academic vocabulary words. Let's imagine a student who is at the **expanding** stage of language proficiency, and who is a fluent reader when reading fiction, is reading this text. The student will likely be able to decode the text but have no idea what the words mean. It is not possible to gain an understanding of the words from the text without some basis of the concept of the book. For example, if we were to replace every academic vocabulary word in the text with SKIP when reading the following except, it wouldn't make much sense.

> The next step is to survey the area the road will cover. An engineer then prepares a plan that details all the road's major features. Decisions must be made: How many lanes will the road have? Will it have any intersections? Are stop signs or traffic lights required? (from *Remarkable Roads*, Estabrooks, p. 25)

Now, let's read it with SKIP where the academic vocabulary words are.

> The next step is to SKIP the SKIP the road will cover. An SKIP then prepares a SKIP that details all the road's major SKIP. SKIP must be made: How many lanes will the road have? Will it have any SKIP? Are stop signs or SKIP lights SKIP? (Adapted from *Remarkable Roads,* Estabrooks, p. 25)

As you can see, there is not much left to make sense of with the text. Multilingual learners, even students who have been redesignated as fluent English proficient, would not know the concepts that the academic words are related to without some preteaching of the vocabulary. The student might be decoding the passage or an entire page or an entire book but would not understand much of what was decoded. The best way to preteach vocabulary is to discuss the words and how they will be used in context. Focus on rich description, building students' background knowledge during the conversation (Bland, 2013).

High-Frequency Words
for Multilingual Learners

responsibility	various	magazine	scientist
similar	professor	governor	appreciate
red	generation	apply	paint
hurt	complete	wall	contract
chief	insurance	twelve	mathematics
reform	blue	beautiful	sister
tree	improve	operation	environment
promise	source	scene	data
defense	commit	threat	schedule
reduce	indeed	ability	file
animal	fan	prison	expert
balance	wind	size	fish
career	district	deep	range
cancer	direct	extend	amaze
damage	fairly	global	direction
hate	bottom	suffer	central
attorney	civil	seat	mark
average	primary	totally	excite
quote	sentence	conservative	council
model	floor	positive	encourage
quick	network	image	
senior	hey	studio	

Scan the QR code to view the New General Service List of 2,800 words developed by Browne, Culligan, and Phillips (2013).

High-frequency word lists organize the most common words seen in text. Many publishers create their own high-frequency word lists based on how often certain words appear in the texts in their books. But these words are not academic words. The New General Service List is a list of 2,800 words developed by Browne et al. (2013). This is a list of high-frequency words that every multilingual student should know. This list includes words like *cure, dash,* and *passive.* However, while these words are found in academic texts, they are not content-specific words that students might encounter while reading informational text. Students need direct instruction of these words, and you can teach these words as some of the sight words you work with at the reading table. Just remember, that multilingual learners will learn to read the word on sight, but they may not know what the word means, so spend time talking about the words, within text, to build understanding for students.

Browne et al. (2013) have also created an academic word list for students learning English. This word list is created of millions of words (so I didn't put it in the appendix!). The headwords (words at the beginning of categories of words) are words like *utterance, vague, essentially,* and *inhibition.* Many of the words in the headword list are Tier II words discussed by Beck et al. (2013). Beck et al. describe words fitting in three categories or tiers; all three categories are important for multilingual learners. There are Tier I, Tier II, and Tier III words.

TIER WORDS

TIER I WORDS

Tier I words are words that rarely need instruction for students who speak English as their heritage language, as they are part of a person's acquired vocabulary as a child, but multilingual learners will need to learn these words. They will know the words conceptually, as the words will be part of their native language repertoire, but they will need to learn the words in English (Nation, 2001). These are words like *mother, car, and bread.* This is a category of words that you teach multilingual learners when they are new to English and at the **beginning** stage of language acquisition. It is best to teach these words to students new to English using real objects. You can label objects in your classroom to teach the words; you can also use real objects, like miniature objects or other items you bring into the classroom (Early, 2005).

TIER II WORDS

Tier II are words that appear frequently in reading, are part of a mature reader's vocabulary, and are found across a variety of content area texts and genres. These are words that convey concepts—for example, *responsibility, freedom,* and *essential.* They tend to be conceptually difficult for an inexperienced reader (Beck et al., 2013) and for multilingual learners. Older multilingual students may know the words conceptually in their native language; however, younger students may not yet know the concept. For example, *enslaved* may or may not be a word that a student understands the concept of—it would depend on what academic discussions they have been involved in or what type of texts they have read. If a multilingual learner is familiar with the concept of *enslaved*, then he needs to learn the label for the concept of *enslaved*. If a student doesn't understand the concept of *enslaved*, the concept of the word will need to be taught.

TIER III WORDS

Tier III words are words connected to content areas and are specific to certain content areas, such as science and social studies. You will also be teaching them at the reading table when you are using informational texts. Tier III words are words like *herbivorous*, *ape*, and *gorilla*.

All three tiers require direct instruction, especially Tier II and III. The explicit teaching does wonders for helping multilingual learners understand the connective words in informational texts. And with Tier III words, the direct teaching is make or break because comprehension is dependent on understanding the content-specific words.

Word Lists to Know

When I work with teachers, they often look to me to "bless" particular word lists. I understand that desire; there are so many words for students to know, where does one begin? Coxhead (2000) developed an academic word list that is a good guide for words to teach students learning English. This list is called the Academic Word List (see companion website). Remember that the word list does not include the 2,000 most frequent words found in print in English. Starting with this word list is one way to get started teaching words to multilingual learners. But be careful! Teaching words out of context needs to be done in small doses. You can also use word lists to know words to bring into discussion as "stretch" words for students to become familiar with, even if the words don't actually appear in the text.

Recap: Teach vocabulary in context. All that we've covered so far in this chapter comes down to one teaching move: teach vocabulary in context. Even when you select words from the word lists I've mentioned, you are always cognizant of the students at the reading table. You are always using the topics, themes, and text to plan the direct vocabulary instruction because your main goal is to have each learner read *that* text. So following are some summary tips:

- Teach words that are embedded in the texts that you are reading with students or that students are reading on their own.

- Engage students in discussion that makes sense to them and provide vocabulary instruction within text.

- Provide opportunities for meaningful use of the words; teach words in context.

At the reading table, we have a natural opportunity to put the vocabulary we are working on in context: The book provides the context because it is filled with pictures, information, and ideas that connect to the words. For example, in the book *Remarkable Roads,* the book provides pictures that support the words.

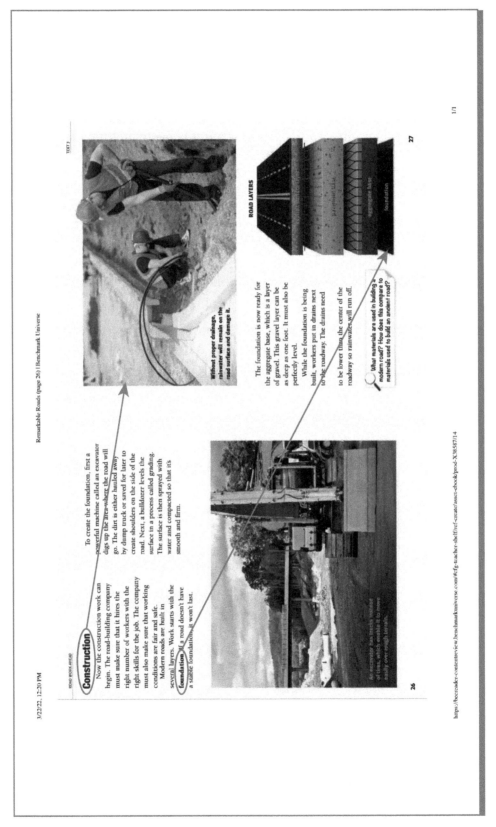

Reprinted with permission of Benchmark Education from the book *Remarkable Roads.*

41

Now, let's turn to preteaching words before reading.

TEACHING WORDS BEFORE READING THE TEXT

Teaching words before reading benefits multilingual learners when it's approached with variety. Day by day, do a mixture of talk, reading, writing, and tactile tasks, like creating word cards, so students stay engaged. The goal is to build context for the words that bring meaning to the text as a whole so that the student can understand both the gist of the text and after repeated reading, the specifics in the text.

- Choose to focus on a small number of the *most important* words to preteach

- Don't preteach a lot of words, as you are teaching the words out of context (you haven't read the book yet to provide any context)

- Focus on the words the student really needs to know to get the gist of the text

- You can focus on deep meaning of the text when teaching words *after* reading the text (see next page) or during a reread

- Make note that when teaching words, you have to do something with the word beyond discussion

- Use visuals to support understanding of new vocabulary

- Using more words multilinguals learners may or may not understand doesn't help in defining new words

As it is said, a picture is worth a thousand words. Pictures, videos, and pantomime go very far in helping students learn new words.

Variations for the Stages of Language Acquisition

To help you plan lessons, following are some ways to differentiate instruction based on the stages of language acquisition.

TEACH IT!

STEPS FOR EMERGENT AND EARLY READERS

You can preteach the vocabulary words during the picture walk of the book
(See the phases of the reading lesson for **emerging** or **developing** readers
in the appendix):

When doing this, follow these steps:

1. Focus on the most important words for students to know to comprehend what
   they are reading. It may only be one to two words that you need to preteach.

2. Stop during the picture walk and explicitly point out the word, read the word
   together, look at the sounds in the word or the word parts, then discuss the word's
   meaning and ask students to put the meaning of the word in their own words.

3. Ask for an example, pointing out pictures or other clues in the text that
   demonstrate the meaning of the word, or ask students what they know about
   the word.

TEACH IT!

STEPS FOR TRANSITIONAL AND FLUENT READERS

When doing this, follow these steps (See the phases of the reading lesson for
expanding and **bridging** readers in the appendix):

1. Preteach a handful of the most important words.

2. Don't focus on a list of words; focus on the concepts and topics that are
   presented in the text and teach the words ahead of time that are going to affect
   students making meaning of the text.

3. Focus on four to five words, maybe less.

4. Explicitly point out the word, read it together, and discuss the word's meaning.

5. Using a tablet or device, show pictures or video that help demonstrate the
   meaning of the word.

6. Ask students to describe the word in their own words,

7. Have students write the word down in a personal dictionary (use a notebook). In
   the personal dictionary, they can write the word, the meaning of the word, and
   the sentence (or part of the sentence) where the word appears.

TEACH IT!

STEPS FOR ENGAGED READERS

When doing this, follow these steps (See the phases of the reading lesson for **bridging** readers, or encourage **expanding** readers to engage in comprehension discussions [see Chapter 9]):

1. Encourage students to note unfamiliar vocabulary as they come across the words during reading.

2. Provide sticky notes for students to flag the pages and note the word.

3. When meeting in group or one on one, ask students to share the unfamiliar words and what they think the word means based on the text. Look up the word definitions, exploring all definitions and finding the right fit.

Activities for Before Reading

- Activate or build prior knowledge through discussion (Blachowicz & Fisher, 2002)
- Examine words during the picture walk
- Teach words to help students get the gist of the word
- Ask students for examples of word meanings
- Create a word bank for the text that is going to be read
- Examine similarities and differences (Marzano et al., 2001)
- Use a personal word dictionary
- Create word cards
- Review word in the index
- Review words in bold in the text
- Creating a preview guide (Peregoy & Boyle, 1997)

TEACHING WORDS
WHILE READING TEXT

Contrary to what many reading programs suggest we do before reading a text with students, we don't want to preteach all the key vocabulary words. As mentioned, you want to preteach *the most important words* to help students get the gist of what they are reading. Why? Because the next level of word instruction is teaching and discussing the word *in context*—the context of reading. The text or book provides a lot of context for the word that is new for students. If we preteach all the words, we rob students of important practice puzzling through words during reading or having you "dip" into the word and define it at point-of-need, as I'll describe next.

Word dipping is when you stop while reading to quickly define a word. You are dipping into the text to focus in on a word, its meaning, and what message the word conveys within the text being read (Laufer, 2010). When word dipping, the students can comprehend not only the word but also what the sentences mean in real time, during the reading.

TEACH IT!

WORD DIPPING

1. The first read through a book or text with multilingual learners will be a choral read.

2. During the choral read, stop and word dip.

3. During a word dip, don't take the time to write the word down. You don't want to stop the flow of the reading.

4. Stop, explain the word, discuss the word's meaning in the text, and then continue reading.

5. Revisit the word after the reading and write the word down, play with the word, or fill out a graphic organizer about the word.

6. When focusing on the word while reading, have students put their finger under the word, focus on the word, and say the word together.

7. Then discuss the word for just long enough to provide understanding of the word. This is done through providing examples.

8. Ask students if they have other examples or explanations of the word.

Fast Mapping

Fast mapping is the unconscious action our memory takes when we first being to learn a word. Our brains create a meaning structure to grapple with a new word, and this happens very quickly. When we first encounter a word, our brains will map some information about the word and with repeated exposure, we will map more meaning of the word (Carey, 1978). We provide repeated encounters of the word when teaching vocabulary after reading the text.

Fast mapping happens when we make connections to a word and then continue reading, allowing the context of the word use in the text to provide more understanding, which in turn adds to the map in our brains. For example, I was reading Anna Quindlen's *Alternate Side*; on page 117, this sentence appears: "That first year the Nolans lived on the block, when she felt she was still auditioning to be a block habitué, Nora has asked Edward Fenstermacher if they had even missed a year, but he said no, never. . . . " Now, when I read this sentence, I had never seen the word *habitué* before, but I tried mapping the word quickly for myself. I noted that part of the word was *habit* as in *habitation*. So I made a connection that *habitué* meant something about living in a place. This all happened so quickly that I just kept reading. I didn't learn *habitué* to the point that it became part of my vocabulary. I just connected to it quickly to bring meaning to what I was reading.

Once you model fast mapping often with students, they will begin to do this on their own.

TEACH IT!

FAST MAPPING

Have students ask

- What word parts do I know?

- What other words does the word look like?

- Is the word like other words I know?

- How does this information connect to what I already know is happening in the text?

- Do I need to look up the word in a dictionary?

- Should I write the word down in my bilingual dictionary? (Yes! Bilingual dictionaries are very helpful for students at the bridging and reaching levels.)

Using Context to Figure Out Words

Students can also use the context of the text to figure out a word's meaning. Let's look at the example I gave from Anna Quindlen's book again. As I worked through figuring out the meaning of *habitué,* I went back and reread the paragraph above it. The paragraph before the one where *habitué* appeared was about the Nolans moving to the block in the neighborhood. So, putting that knowledge together with my guess about the word during fast mapping clinched the meaning for me. I also noted that my thinking about *habitué* made sense in the syntax of the sentence. *Habitué* is a description of a type of person living somewhere.

TEACH IT!

USING CONTEXT

Help multilingual students to figure out words using context doesn't mean just telling them, "Use the sentences around the word to figure out what the word means." You must practice this a lot with them to help:

- Model by thinking aloud about your thought processes

- Engage students in similar processes by prompting them to think through figuring out the word meanings (Laufer, 2010)

It could also be that there are other words in the sentences around the unknown key word that the students are not 100 percent sure about the meaning, so using the context can be difficult. When this happens, I recommend to students to reread a whole paragraph before the word if the word seems to be key to understanding the gist of the text. (Remember you can revisit the word later if needed.) If using web-based text, students can also use a hyperlink to look up the meaning of the word quickly. I don't usually have students stop and look up a word manually in a dictionary because it disrupts the flow of the reading, but using a hyperlink is quick. Students could also refer to the index if needed.

Word Forms

Multilingual students need multiple opportunities to work with words and with what Laufer (2010) calls *word forms.* Word forms are phrases that are common and repeated in text; for example, *a dilemma, compare and contrast,* or *the author's opinion is.* Guide students to look for these types of repeating phrases to help them figure out the meaning of other unknown words in sentences.

TEACH IT!

WORD FORMS

Steps to using the context to figure out the word can include the following:

1. Stop and think; what part of speech is this word? Is it a noun? A verb? An adjective? Decide what it is so you know what you are predicting (it doesn't help to think of possible adjectives if the word is a noun).

2. What do the sentences before and after the word share? What information is being shared? In light of this information, what might this word mean?

3. What is the paragraph before the word about? Does this provide any clues to what the word means?

4. Use a hyperlink to look up the word meaning. Check the index.

5. If really necessary, look up the word in an online dictionary.

Questioning Strategies for Figuring Out a Word

Multilingual students need validation to know that they have the power to figure out word meanings. They can work on routines for helping themselves figure out a word so that they are facing a large number of words in which they are fuzzy about the meaning (Carlo et al., 2004).

TEACH IT!

Have students ask themselves:

1. Did I check what the text would be about before I started reading? (Look at pictures, title, headings.)

2. Did I check the headings and subheadings to make sure I know what the section I am reading is about?

3. What do I already know about the subject/problem/point the text is discussing? Does this help me figure out what it says?

Activities for During Reading

- Word dipping
- Fast mapping
- Using context to figure out words
- Verbally making associations to a word
- Rereading to read the word in context
- Checking the word's definition
- Using questioning strategies

TEACHING WORDS AFTER READING THE TEXT

When teaching vocabulary after reading a text, you can focus on definition-building lessons. Through the two types of activities I am going to introduce in this section, you are guiding students to focus on the deeper meaning of the words and words that connect together. One way to do this is to use semantic maps. When using a semantic map, you will be helping students connect images in their minds with words and their thinking. You will be helping students use multiple images to understand what a word means. Students create images in their minds when we discuss the meanings of words and the concepts the word represents. For example, if I were to describe *responsibility*, I might say to students, "responsibility is when you help your mom or dad around the house. Do you take out the trash? Do you help cook? What do you do? Let's talk about it; all these things that we do are our *responsibilities*." When we talk, read aloud, and show students video or pictures on the web, children begin to see for themselves, in their minds, what we are presenting both verbally and in images. Then, as they hear more information, children's schema about certain words will become more developed.

Using Semantic Maps

To begin with a semantic map, I begin with what I call a wheel map; I write the target word in the middle of a circle drawn on a paper or screen. I might say, "When I say a word or think of a word, a flood of images comes to my mind. I try to focus on one of the images to help me remember the meaning of a word. I can write that down or draw a picture. Today we are going to learn some new words. Let's check them out!" I would write a word on the map and then describe what the word means or perhaps show images or a video on the internet. Then brainstorming with students, I would write words that describe the concept of the word in the circle around the word. I can also draw pictures or copy and paste pictures onto the screen.

Wheel Map

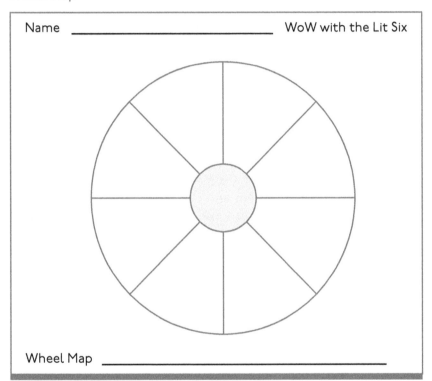

Name _____ WoW with the Lit Six

Wheel Map _____

Comparing and Contrasting Topics in Text

Comparing and contrasting topics in text is a type of categorization. Using a Venn diagram, I put two topics on the graphic organizer, one over each bubble, and then have students list words that describe each topic or idea from the text, writing the words in the bubble. In the middle of the Venn diagram, I write words that describe any point in the text where the words come together with meaning; see the following example.

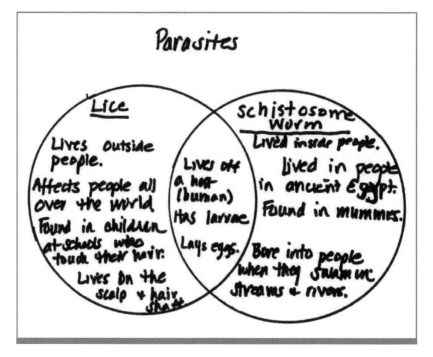

You can compare and contrast themes in a book, topics in an informational text, or a bit idea that an informational text is about. For example, if I were reading a book with students on the digestive system and the book discussed body parts, I might write *stomach* on one side of the Venn diagram and *intestines* on the other side of the Venn. Working with students, I could write words that describe *stomach* and *intestines* and in the middle write *digestion;* see the above example.

Activities for After Reading

- Semantic maps

- Comparing and contrasting topics

- Define words as a group

- Create word banks

- Categorize words

- Do a word shakedown—write down as many words as possible that connect to the word in some way via memories or experiences of students

- Using a Frayer model (Dazzeo & Rao, 2020), define the word in the student's own words; describe examples of the word using other words and phrases; describe nonexamples of the word using words and phrases; and use the word in a sentence

WORD	EXAMPLES
microburst	miniture tornado extreme storm little twisters strong wind
DEFINITION Upside-down, short-lived tornadoes	small storms only covering 3 miles or less
SENTENCE or PICTURE The mircoburst made the plane crash.	NON-EXAMPLES Calm air large storms covering more than 3 miles no wind no rain

- Map a word focusing on the definition, a picture or sketch representing the word, and the function of the word (adjective, noun, verb, adverb)

Looking Ahead

This chapter was all about expanding students' vocabularies. I imagine as you read it, there wasn't a single activity that wouldn't work for even your most advanced students. All children benefit from scaffolding, visual props, and connecting new words to known content. So I want you to feel confident that you can bring students to the reading table who are a mix of multilingual students and students who need scaffolding. With multilingual students, sure, at the reading table, you are sometimes most watchful of them. You might notice confusion and draw a word or do a concept map for all kids or coach them first and for more minutes. In the next chapter, we look at how to how to help students work with words and word parts to develop a greater understanding.

CHAPTER EIGHT

Word Work

iStock.com/FatCamera

Expanding multilingual students' vocabularies is vital, empowering, and a make-or-break move when it comes to teaching reading. As you saw in the oral language and vocabulary chapters, there are lots of ways to do that. Yet what's also true is that teaching new words should be second in line to teaching *about* new words (Carlo et al., 2004). When we teach about words, we teach various kinds of information that help students figure out the word meanings for themselves. Academic texts have many complex words in them, so when students know some of the common prefixes, roots, and suffixes, they will be better able to figure out the meaning of words while reading and grow their vocabularies (Freeman & Freeman, 2014).

Serendipitously, teaching of word parts tucks so easily into what we are *doing at the reading table.* After all, we have just twenty minutes a day to spend with groups of students to go deep on a few strategies. Within this context, teaching word parts makes sense.

Common Challenges

We want students to learn about phonemes as readers to help them decode. Phonemes are units of sound that help students sound out words. As we explored in the phonics chapter, students use this knowledge of letters and sounds to decode words and to write or spell them, too. When multilingual learners are in the **entering** and **expanding** stages, decoding work should take up a big part of the phonics instruction. A critical next step is recognizing when learners have sufficient decoding abilities such that instruction should shift to working with words. Continuing to teach phonemes will not help students with understanding the text because phonemes don't carry any meaning (Rasinski et al., 2011). The other common challenge, which is related, is that in general, multilingual students aren't getting robust enough vocabulary instruction. At the reading table, we want to ramp up word work so students expand their skills for figuring out unknown words—and when they can do that, they expand their vocabularies on their own. Again, all the memorizing of word lists and spelling quizzes won't help the learning stick.

Attributes of Dynamic Word Work

Working with words overlaps with—or is a subset of— spelling and vocabulary instruction, and so the principle of teaching within a meaningful context holds true. The best way to expand vocabulary is teaching words and word parts connected to a text, as you discern its meaning and have ample opportunities for meaningful use.

Dynamic instruction at the reading table also balances teaching students the **process** and **structure** of language. These are considered the two prongs of language instruction for multilingual students. When we focus on the *process* of learning language, this means we are providing students with opportunities for speaking and listening through discussion, explicit language instruction, or spontaneous language acquisition through unplanned interaction. When we focus on teaching the structure of language, we are focusing on morphology—on how words are put together; new language structures; and form and content (Miramontes et al., 1997). If we focus on one prong more than the other, students' language acquisition will not be maximized (Akhavan, 2007).

In describing this two-prong approach, Cazden (2001) states that one prong gives multilingual students opportunities to practice in authentic conversations and writing. The second prong gives students direct instruction on conventions of form. Students need to be explicitly taught the skills of writing words and how words are put together, but it's *how* this is taught that is important (Akhavan, 2007).

Students need

- Active engagement

- Authentic conversation

- Talking—and talking often about words

- No worksheet fill-in-the-blank exercises

- Scaffolded lessons with diagrams, pictures, videos, and other items to make words real and concrete (Cazden, 2017)

Begin by Teaching Compound Words

Compound words appear in multiple types of texts that students read, including leveled text, decodable texts, high-interest texts aligned to grade levels, and content area texts. When students understand that a compound word is made up of two words that carry meaning, they can figure out what the word means and how the word brings meaning to the sentence and the paragraph they are reading. Remember that teaching about words is done to teach students how to determine the meaning of what they are reading.

It is helpful to begin teaching compound words by teaching compounds that are made up of two syllables. (See companion website for a list of common two-syllable words.) Students will need to know the meaning of each small word that makes up the compound word, and multilingual learners, once they are able to speak fairly fluently in an interpersonal situation, will

online resources

likely know many of these words. This occurs at approximately the expanding phase of language acquisition. Remember that students at the expanding phase have good control of conversational English, as long as the conversations are not academic and they have learned quite a bit of basic vocabulary in English. Here are some examples of two-syllable compound words made up of small words that students would likely know the meaning of:

- bedroom
- backpack
- ballpark
- carsick
- daytime
- football
- pancake
- playhouse

- raindrop
- softball
- stoplight
- taillight
- toothpaste
- upstairs
- weekday

How to Teach Compound Words

In the lesson sequences for the work at the reading table (Chapter 4), I note that students may be working on word work. You can teach compound words as part of word work. Remember that the teaching of skills doesn't take over the time students have for reading. Keep the teaching of skills quick and engaging.

TEACH IT!

To teach compound words, follow these guidelines:

1. Write the word in a sentence on a small whiteboard or on chart paper near the reading table. You might write

   a. *I stopped my car at the stoplight.*

2. Read the sentence to the students while pointing to the words.

3. Move your hand *under* the words as you read. Read the sentence a couple of times if necessary.

4. Discuss the sentence and read it again. Read it enough times to make sure students understand the meaning of the sentence.

5. Focus on the compound word. Discuss how the word is made up of two words and when the two words come together, they have a new and specific meaning. So in *stoplight,* you might say that you stop at the light but that a *stoplight* is the specific machine that changes color, and the word is the name for the machine. You can sketch a quick picture of stoplight or show a stoplight on a device so you can be sure students understand what you are talking about.

Teaching Two-Syllable Compound Words

During the word work part of the lesson, you will be teaching words that may not be in the book. Word work needs to be taught in a systematic manner, and it is not dependent on the words that appear in the book. You can use the sections of this book as a way to approach your sequence. We don't rely on the book to lead our word work because students need clear instruction aligned to what they need to know about how words work. Of course, as we come across words in the texts we read with students, we can point out the words or word patterns that we have been working on. Remember that you are teaching the skills as part of the teaching sequences in lessons presented in Chapter 4, page 68, so the word work is just a section of the lesson. It might only take five minutes.

For a list of common compound words, visit **resources.corwin.com/ smallgroupreadingMLL** online resources.

You can also teach compound words by writing a few more compound words in sentences on a board or chart paper and ask students if they can find the compound word. To make it easier at first, make sure you are focusing on two-syllable compound words.

General guidelines at the reading table and beyond include the following:

- As you write sentences and have students identify the compound words, spend some time talking about the words.

- Write the individual words down and discuss the meaning of each word, sketching a picture of the word if needed or inding a picture of the meaning of the words on the internet and display on a device.

(Continued)

(Continued)

- Then follow up with discussing the meaning of the words put together and sketch a picture or display a picture or video of the meaning of the compound word. Ensure that you are not just discussing the word orally; multilingual learners need context to understand vocabulary, and just talking about word meaning is not enough. You need to show the meaning of the words through pictures, visuals, and even actions—like pantomime.

TEACH IT!

Think of this process in four steps:

1. Write a sentence using the compound word.

2. Identify the compound word and write it down by itself. Write the word as two words put together by a + sign: *stop + light*.

3. Discuss the two words in the compound word, defining each as necessary. Use visuals!

4. Rewrite the compound word down and define the word, discussing how both words come together to make new meaning. Use visuals!

Going Beyond Teaching Two-Syllable Compound Words

Once students know many two-syllable compound words, you can begin teaching multisyllabic compound words. These words are a bit more complicated as they have multiple parts and may be written with prefixes or suffixes. Some compounds are separated by a hyphen, and others, called open compounds, have a space between them but are considered a compound word because the two words together create the meaning of a new word. Now, remember that with multilingual students we are teaching meaning when focusing on compound words, not just being able to decode the word, so it makes sense to teach open compounds as well as closed compounds.

See the companion website for a sample list of multisyllabic compound words. Multisyllabic compound words including open compound words like these:

basketball	credit card
neighborhood	database
screwdriver	living room
supermarket	coffee cup
motorcycle	long-term
fingernail	up-to-date
stepping-stone	deep-fried

Teaching Open and Hyphenated Words

Some hyphenated and open compound words may be tricky for multilingual learners. This is because the word combination meaning relates to language that is colloquial and they might not be familiar with the phrase. When I say "hyphenated compound word," I am referring to words like *old-school, well-thought-out* and *mother-in-law.* Open hyphenated words are two words written separately, but they are connected for meaning. For example, *ice cream, mountain bike,* and *real estate.*

Scan the QR code to see Merriam-Webster's new words added to the dictionary in 2022.

We need to be explicit and teach multilingual learners these sayings and expressions. You can teach them when colloquialisms appear in the text you are reading with the students. You can also teach them after working on compound words and students are getting the hang of compound words. Find hyphenated compound words or open compound words by looking through books in your classroom or do a quick Google search. Over time, language changes, and new compound words are created by people and how they commonly talk. Eventually, words are used enough that official dictionaries, like *Merriam-Webster,* recognize the words and include them in printed and online dictionaries. Compound words added in 2019 include *deep state* and *pickle ball.* Remember that the reason that new words are added is because they represented new meanings in our modern culture and world. For all students and multilingual learners especially, word learning sticks when the instruction is focused on the meaning and the context in which these words are used.

For terms like *sweet tooth* or *high-speed,* the meaning cannot be determined just by reading the words creating the compound word. The words may be expressing meaning about a phenomena or condition. These words will take more explanation. It helps to give multiple examples in a sentence so the student can develop conceptual understanding of the word by reading the entire sentence or sentences to get the gist of the meaning. For example, *sweet tooth* might be used like this:

I ate too much candy last night. My sweet tooth made me do it!

TEACH IT!

The steps to teaching open or hyphenated compound words are as follows:

1. Write the compound word on the board and discuss the open space or hyphen (whatever is appropriate based on the word you write).

2. Discuss the two words in the compound word, defining each as necessary. Use visuals to define the words. Write the word as two words put together by an imaginary + sign: *pickle (+) ball*.

3. Discuss how the two words are connected together to create a new meaning or a new idea, thought, or phenomenon. For example, *pickle ball* means not a ball made of pickles but rather a type of game.

4. Define the open or hyphenated compound word, discussing how both words come together to make a new meaning. Use visuals!

MORPHOLOGY

Ready for a blast from your past, in education classes? I use the term *morphology* because it's a helpful reminder that when acquiring English, all students are learning a morphophonemic language, meaning that the word spellings reflect the sound structure and the word structure (Apel & Henbest, 2016). This is important for students to know so they can feel like they are mastering English—they can be in control of their language learning. So I might say something like, "English has little sounds in it that build into bigger sounds that create words. We are going to think about the little sounds so that English makes more sense." The instructional implications are that we *integrate* phonics, spelling, and word work because the nature of English dictates this holistic approach.

Morphemes: Morphemes are the smallest unit of language that carry meaning. Morphemes can be base words or free morphemes (*go* and *see)* or affixes or bound morphemes (prefixes and suffixes). Morphological awareness affects students reading and spelling abilities (Nagy et al., 2006). When working with multilingual learners, teaching prefixes, suffixes, and base words helps them decode words and also helps them with spelling words. However, the most important thing that increasing students' morphological understanding can do is help students understand what the words mean (Kieffer & Lesaux, 2011; Kruk & Bergman, 2013).

Prefixes and suffixes: Students will encounter prefixes and suffixes in their reading. As they grow as readers and the books they are reading are more complex, their need to know prefixes and suffixes intensifies. Usually, in emergent and early reader texts, the words are simpler. Words students will certainly see in texts have suffixes that change the meaning of the base word: *-s, -ed, -ing, -ly.* Multilingual learners need help in pronouncing words with suffixes. They might read *work/ed* for *worked.* It is correctly pronounced *workt.* They need help in knowing how the suffixes are pronounced. The suffix *-ed* is pronounced either */id/, /t/,* or */d/.* As we know, the *e* is silent, but multilingual learners working on decoding words won't know that; they will need practice to remember how to correctly pronounce the word with the suffix. It is the sound that is important, not the letter.

As students develop as readers and move from **early** readers to **transitional** readers, they will encounter vocabulary that is more complex (as discussed in Chapter 7). Students will need to know how prefixes and suffixes change the meaning of words so that they can break words up when they encounter them in text to help them with the meaning of the words. Nagy and Anderson (1984) note that beginning in third grade, approximately 60 percent of words that students see in texts are constructed of prefixes, suffixes, and roots. Manyak et al. (2018) have developed a list of forty-one prefixes and suffixes that students in grades 3 through 6 should know. These are also the affixes that multilingual learners need to know. But there is a caveat: Don't simply teach these words to multilingual learners out of context, not connected to text. They need a lot of context.

You can teach the words aside from text if you are having fun with the prefixes and suffixes; perhaps, you play word games.

You can also pull words from the texts you are reading with the students and then create a word bank that includes other words with the same prefix or suffix.

Teaching Roots

Effective word-learners break words up into meaningful parts and then check them against the meaning of the text and their background knowledge (Anderson & Nagy, 1992; Freyd & Baron, 1982). All students need instruction in understanding meaningful word parts like prefixes, suffixes, and root words, but multilingual learners need very specific instruction in the meaningful parts of words as they have had less exposure to English overall.

Visit the companion website for more resources on teaching roots at **resources.corwin.com/smallgroupreadingMLL**

Biemiller and Slonim (2001) determined that students learn approximately six hundred root words each year from infancy to the end of elementary school. If students are multilingual learners, they have been developing root words—in their primary language. So once they start acquiring English, they will need direct instruction to accelerate their learning of word parts. They are in essence playing catch-up, as they won't have a bank of root words in English the way children who are native English speakers do. They also need time playing with language, as children learn a lot of language by playing with words, singing, and through reading (Carlisle, 2010; Kieffer & Lesaux, 2011; Rasinski et al., 2011).

TEACH IT!

You *can* teach prefixes and suffixes on their own (not using vocabulary from the text students are reading) by building words and then exploring the meaning.

1. Post a chart with a column of prefixes, a column of simple root words, and a column of suffixes.

2. Build words by choosing a root and then adding a prefix, a suffix, or both. Invite students to write the word down on a whiteboard.

3. Have students erase the prefix or suffix and read the root. Define the root together.

4. Have students rewrite the prefix or suffix and then read and define the word.

5. To define the words for multilingual learners, remember PAGES to contextualize the words for the students:

- P: pictures or drawings

- A: acting out the word

- G: graphics

- E: easy—make the word easy to understand

- S: seeing a video

Teaching Latin and Greek Roots

Base words are considered root words; they are one in the same. Some of our base words come from old languages, including Latin and Greek, and these are known as Greek and Latin roots. Students in Grades 4 and up need instruction on Greek and Latin roots as they begin learning more content, as they will see academic words with Greek and Latin roots. That said, keep in mind that having students memorize a list of root words and making up words they don't understand with prefixes and suffixes is not what I am talking about. What students can do is play with the words and think about what they mean out of context (or discussed on their own and not in the context of a book or text). Word play with roots is one thing you can do to help students understand roots. You can also point them out to students as you come across Tier II or Tier III (see Chapter 7) words in texts.

Greek or Latin roots. Most academic words and most challenging multisyllabic words in English have Greek or Latin roots (Rasinski et al., 2011). In fact, 80 percent of the words in English that come from other languages have a Greek or Latin root and make us 60 percent of our language (Henry, 1993). English language learners can use Greek and Latin roots to give them clues to the meaning of the academic word they encounter in text. Remember that teaching word parts to increase students' language acquisition is about focusing on *meaning*; we teach the word parts to help students figure out what the text is saying, not just to pronounce a word or decode a word. English language learners' success in content area reading depends on comprehension.

Many years ago, Brown (1947) created a Greek and Latin word list that is still very helpful today. This list (see figure that follows) contains 14 root words (12 Latin and 2 Greek). These root words, combined with 20 common prefixes or suffixes, can make up to 100,000 words (Henry, 1990; Rasinski et al., 2011). If students learn the meaning of the roots, they will have clues to the meaning of many words.

Brown's 14 Roots

No.	Root	Meaning	Origin	Example
I	tent, ten, tin, tain	To have, hold	Latin	tenant maintain continually retain
2	mit, miss, mitt	To send	Latin	omit permissible commit
3	cap, capit, cip, cept	To take, seize	Latin	capital caption emancipate discipline
4	fer	To bear, carry	Latin	suffer infer
5	sta, stat, sist	To stand (on), remain,	Latin	constant distant insist
6	graph, gram	To write	Greek	paragraph autograph
7	log, ology	Science	Greek	pharmacology biology
8	spect	To look, see	Latin	spectacle aspect

No.	Root	Meaning	Origin	Example
9	plic, plex, ply	To fold, bend	Latin	duplicate complicated replicate
10	tens, tend, tent	To stretch and strain	Latin	tense ontensity intently
11	duc, duct	To lead, make	Latin	reproduction conduct
12	pos, pon	To put, place	Latin	compose position oppose
13	fac, fic, fact	To make, do	Latin	fiction factual artifact
14	scribe, script	To write	Latin	transcribe describe manuscript

Adapted from Brown, 1947.

Help Students Think Conceptually

Students will need to spend time understanding what a root is and how the root provides meaning to a word. It is sometimes conceptual and not literal. For example, the roots *plic, plex,* and *pli* mean to fold or bend. Now the words made up of these roots, like *duplicate,* don't seem to have anything to do with *fold* or *bend.* So one needs to think of the idea conceptually—when something is duplicated, it is folded, making a replica of itself. Or consider the word *discipline,* with the roots *cap, capit,* and *cip, cept,* which mean to seize or to take. *Discipline* is the process of training someone to follow rules of order; they seize or take the rules as they learn them.

When you are working with multilingual learners at the reading table and you are choosing to teach root words, you will only have a few minutes to focus on root word instruction, as you have other activities to do at the reading table as well.

This means that you need to get the most learning out of the instruction you are implementing:

- You can explore different roots and their meaning and then discuss some words that are made of the roots that you are working with (see the appendix for a root word list).

- You can also take apart the word and discuss the prefix or suffix, if there is one, and how the affix adds to the meaning of the word.

- You can also highlight a handful of words, three to five, in an informational or content text that you are reading with the students and check out the roots in those words and discuss the meaning of the word.

- You can post the fourteen common root words, see pages 166–67 and their meanings in the classroom in a place that is easily visible for students when they are reading independently so that they can use the roots of words to begin working through the meaning of words they come across and that are giving them trouble.

Teach the roots that appear in words by focusing on meaning. For multilingual learners, building words from prefixes, suffixes, and roots or thinking of words with the same root in them may not be very successful; depending on their vocabularies, they may simply just not know enough academic words yet. So focus on playing with the words to figure out meaning. One of the best activities is Read and Reason, which follows (adapted from Rasinski et al., 2011).

TEACH IT!

To engage students in Read and Reason, you

1. During reading, when or if students come to a new word with a root that you have been teaching, stop and discuss.

2. Write the word on a whiteboard or chart. Invite students to examine the word and see if they can identify the root.

3. Discuss the meaning of the root.

4. Look at the word in the context of the text again and reread the sentence aloud, stopping to discuss the root meaning and how it relates to the meaning of the sentence.

5. Refocus students back on the word on the board, reinforce the meaning of the word. Ask students to share their thinking about how the word is used in the sentence.

KEEP IT VISUAL

ADDITIONAL COMMON ROOTS AND THEIR MEANINGS

capere: capt, cap, cept (take, seize)

tener: ten, tent, tin, tain (hold, have)

mittere: mit, miss, (send)

stare: sta, sis, sti (stand)

ferre: fer (bear, yield, carry)

graphein: graph (write)

legein: leg, lig, lect, log (say, study of)

specere: spec, spic, spect (see)

plicare: plic, pli, ply (to fold, bend)

tendere: tend, tens, tent (stretch)

ducure: duc, duct (lead)

ponere: pos, pon (place, put)

facere: fac, fee, fic, fact (do, make, put)

scriber: scrib, script (write)

Used with permission by Rasinski (2010).

Teaching Cognates (Spanish)

Multilingual learners can learn the meaning of words in English through the study of cognates. Cognates are words that come from the same root, so if a student knows a word in one language, he can figure out the meaning of the word in English (Freeman & Freeman, 2014). For some cognates in some languages, the words are nearly identical. A student who is a Spanish speaker and knows *imposible* can learn *impossible* in English by understanding that the words look the same and mean the same thing. Because a large number of English academic words have a Latin base, students who speak languages derived from Latin, like Spanish, may already know the words, and the meaning can just transfer to English (Montelongo et al., 2011).

TEACH IT!

To teach cognates, you can

- Have students identify cognates in the informational texts you are reading with students and create a cognate word list, listing the word in English and then the word in the students' primary language.

- Create a cognate personal dictionary, and students can keep it with them while reading and add words to it as they see them in text.

- Create and grow cognate lists after reading several books, and once you have several cognates on the list, you can work with the cognates for a few minutes, having students categorize them.

Students can categorize cognates by words with the same spelling or words with predictable variations in spelling. Students can also categorize the words in your cognate list by suffixes and spelling patterns of the suffixes. Playing with the words and categorizing words are excellent ways for students to become familiar with cognates, and these can rapidly increase their academic vocabularies (Johnston et al., 2000). A short cognate list in Spanish is on the [online resources] companion website. You can find cognate lists for other languages by doing a Google search of a student's primary language and cognates in English.

TEACH IT!

To teach cognates' bring attention to the words and discuss them:

- Find cognates in the informational texts students are reading.
- Add cognates to a word bank or word list.
- Talk about the cognate, discussing the similarity of spelling or the suffix pattern of the cognate.

Caveats to Teaching Word Structure for Cues to Meaning

As we've seen throughout this chapter, students can benefit from a variety of swift, playful activities with words—or rather, taking words apart and then putting them together to build meaning. In addition to my usual mantra of *make it meaningful,* there are a couple of particular caveats I want you to be aware of.

First, teaching word part clues can be useful to help students figure out unknown words, but it needs to be used judiciously (Freeman & Freeman, 2014). Sometimes, focusing on word parts is not helpful. Let me explain both points of view. Knowing word parts and chunking words into parts can be really helpful when the word part gives a clue to meaning. For example, when teaching compound words, breaking the words in the compound word apart helps students to figure out the meaning. Also, looking for small words in a big word might help students sound out a word, but it doesn't always work to figure out a word's meaning. Take *cardboard* for example. If students know what a card is, they might be confused when thinking of a playing card and a board together. They would need to know that *card* refers to a type paper, not a playing card. However, with *daybreak* it might be easier for students to figure out the meaning. They would probably know the meaning of *day,* and they could likely figure out that *break* was breaking the darkness, so *daybreak* means *sunrise.*

Confusion can also occur when students try to figure out a word's meaning by looking at the small words in a big word. Take *hotel* for example. Students could be really confused about the meaning of *hotel* if they identified *hot* as a small word in a big word and then were thinking of something hot. So teaching students to look for small words in big words or breaking apart compound words doesn't work best for multilingual learners if they don't know the meaning of the words individually. What works better is to teach them the meaning of prefixes, suffixes, and common roots.

WHEN TEACHING WORD PARTS—FOCUS ON THE MEANING INSTEAD OF THE PART

- Confusion can also occur when students try to figure out a word's meaning by looking at the small words in a big word.

- Focus on the meaning of the parts of a word, as in smaller words that make up compound words and Greek and Latin roots.

- Word work is playful, swift, and meaningful. We want students to pick up our curiosity about the patterns and curveballs of the English language. When combined with talk, vocabulary instruction, and the daily delight in noticing the book authors' facility with language, multilingual learners will feel more confident in reading, writing, and talking in English as well.

Looking Ahead

Word work is playful, swift, and meaningful. We want students to pick up our curiosity about the patterns and curve balls of the English language. When combined with talk, vocabulary instruction, and the daily delight in noticing the book authors' facility with language, multilingual learners will feel more confident in reading, writing, and talking in English as well. Next, we focus on developing comprehension at the reading table.

CHAPTER NINE

Comprehension

iStock.com/Chinnapong

When I think of multilingual learners at the reading table working through text and stopping to talk about what they have read, images flash through my mind of students excited to share, eyes shining, nearly cutting each other off mid-sentence because they are so eager. The air has buoyancy and is alive with students thinking. The work at the reading table is not drudgery. It is a time to engage about thoughts and ideas and to feel accomplished because of having read an exciting or interesting text.

Common Challenges

All too often, I see multilingual learners at the reading table silent, laboriously working their way through text that is not engaging for them or being timid because they don't know the words to express their thoughts. I want all students to lean into their reading and lean into the conversations they can have about their reading, whether they are communicating by discussing ideas or drawing pictures to show what they cannot yet express.

Comprehension instruction for multilingual learners is not a quiet activity. Rather than picturing in your mind students reading a text and quietly answering questions about a text or writing in a journal, I want you to think of students involved in lively academic conversations about what they have been reading. If no one is talking in your group, no one is acquiring language. Students should be writing about their reading and recording their thinking, but the conversation comes first, and the writing may happen in groups or with a partner.

Attributes of Dynamic of Comprehension Instruction

Before we delve into the comprehension strategies you can teach, let's talk about the text students are reading. Teaching multilingual learners to read well and understand what they read means we value and honor our students' backgrounds and make their cultural background most important and relevant in our classrooms (Akhavan, 2019). Students need to see themselves in the texts they read (Muhammad, 2020). Therefore, we need to realize and understand how our personal biases can infiltrate our instruction without even realizing it. We may not be thinking about the race, culture, backgrounds, or heritage language of the people in the books we are presenting to students. We do need to focus on this. Where and how are the people who look like your students represented in books and text?

Be a Culturally Responsive Teacher

At the reading table, use texts about famous or well-known people from cultural backgrounds and races similar to your students. Also use texts that feature people outside of the student makeup. By doing this—bringing in books about people outside of what the mainstream culture focuses on—we become even more inclusive. We transmit the values, norms, beliefs, and knowledge of our students' home cultural backgrounds so as not to try to replace students' backgrounds with mainstream culture but to add to their cultural backgrounds (De Jong & Harper, 2005; Romero-Little, 2010). You can prepare to do this by learning about your students' cultural backgrounds.

Three Guiding Principles

If you are reading this book, no doubt you are a culturally responsive teacher. If you ever wonder if you are doing enough for your multilingual students in terms of text selection, use the following three guidelines for honoring students' race, cultures, norms, and values.

1. Look at the reading materials available to your students and see if pictures of people similar, or like them, are represented in text. If not, seek out books that do portray people of your students' cultural backgrounds. You might even want to think of purchasing books or texts (you can always appeal to the administration to fund the project) to ensure students have access to culturally responsive texts.

2. Incorporate activities that mirror and honor the communication patterns that students are often involved in at home.

3. Find books about students' favorite topics and interests.

Begin With Awareness of the Group for Comprehension Conversations

Engage students in conversation about their reading to develop reading comprehension and develop language acquisition in English. However, keep in mind that some of your students may thrive during boisterous open-ended discussions; others may be very uncomfortable even in low-key book and text conversations. One reason they may be uncomfortable is their acquisition level of English, but another reason is the cultural norms of communication that they know and connect with daily at home. You can do a bit of research on the communication and relationship styles of your students' cultures and take these into consideration when organizing group talk about books and texts. Conversation norms vary culture by culture.

At the reading table, you will be teaching comprehension and developing your students' language acquisition levels. Through oral language discussions and written responses, your students will

- Build their academic vocabulary and deepen their cognitive language abilities. Cognitive language abilities are the schema, language structures, and language knowledge that your students develop about academic text structures (Cummins, 1979).

- Facilitate group discussions to foster comprehension of text. Your students may come from a culture where it is common to work together and will thrive during group conversations. Others may not be used to group work and may want to sit quietly and take it in. You will need to navigate the differences between students while still helping students work toward group comprehension conversations (McIntyre, 2010).

How to Group Conversations Based on Level of Acquisition

Over the course of days and weeks, you want to keep small group membership flexible, moving students around so they develop relationships with everyone. Here are some pointers for when you want to group students based on their level of language acquisition (see pages 38–42 in Chapter 2 for more on these stages).

- Students at the **entering** phase of language acquisition in English may be focused on participating in group conversations by making connections between the text you are working with and the vocabulary you have been teaching.

- Students at the **emerging** and **developing** stages will be building their personal communication skills during comprehension conversations, and you will be developing their academic language knowledge through vocabulary instruction and academic discussions.

- Students at the **expanding** level of language acquisition may be able to chatter away with peers informally but struggle with academic vocabulary, academic language, and discussions.

- Students at the **bridging** and **reaching** levels of language acquisition will be able to take a deeper dive with academic discussions; while they may still make errors in semantics and syntax, they will be able to apply and use increasing amounts of academic language in their discussions and in writing.

Make Conversations Visual

Students who are acquiring English find it difficult to track the information you are sharing if you are only talking about texts (Cummins, 2011). They haven't necessarily developed the academic vocabulary yet to focus on the message and the academic language at the same time. To scaffold your instruction, you need to make your oral discussion visual (Gibbons, 2015). For example, a few weeks ago I was visiting Kris Durkin's classroom. She was working with a group of multilingual learners who wanted to know about North and South America based on a sentence in the text about where animals live. She started explaining North and South America, giving lots of details and describing with her hands. I could see that the students still were not quite understanding. I pulled up a map of North and South America on my tablet and handed it to her, and she was able to demonstrate using the map—the visual made the difference, and students chimed in with their ideas about the continents and the animals in their book.

TEACH IT!

To scaffold students with visuals and tactile tools

- Use a graphic organizer—perhaps turn it into a chart—to guide students' thinking and discussion about their text connections.

- Scaffold the students' oral and written responses while making text connections by providing sentence frames. Sentence frames can simply be posted near the teaching table, or you can use a graphic organizer. There are examples of each of these in the sections to follow based on each reading comprehension strategy.

Scaffolding Comprehension

Readers simultaneously extract and construct meaning from text as they read (Wilkinson & Son, 2011). You are doing this right now as you read this paragraph. You are thinking about what I am saying to you, but you are also thinking about what I am saying and how it relates to your personal teaching practices. So you are extracting meaning from my words and constructing meaning as my message relates to your life experiences. In fact, sometimes, you might even have a conversation with me in your head.

- Students don't always know that they are to make meaning of the text, consider the messages the author is presenting, and then think about those messages based on their own knowledge and ideas.

- Students need explicit instruction in comprehension strategies to do this sophisticated memory work (Wharton-McDonald, 2014).

- Teach the comprehension strategies directly during reading instruction and provide lots of time for independent reading for students to practice those strategies.

- Encourage independent reading so students fall in love with reading and then have a purpose for their reading.

- Give them time to think about what they are reading and talk about what they are reading so they can construct meaning that is significant for themselves.

While students who are at the **expanding** and **bridging** levels may be reading fairly well, they are still working on understanding the text while learning a language. So they may not know the meaning of all the words that are used in the text or understand with clarity the message of the author. Supporting multilingual learners with comprehension instruction enables students to emulate what skilled readers do and enhances their comprehension (Pressley et al., 1995).

Whatever comprehension strategy you are encouraging students to try, they will need time to think about it. They may not be able to come up with their thoughts in English in a few seconds like students who speak English as their heritage language:

- Give the students a little think time; have them talk their connection over with a peer in order to practice their oral language skills, and then they can write their thinking down.

- Encourage the development of listening, speaking, and writing along with the reading (the four modes of language).

- Working with listening, speaking, reading, and writing in one lesson helps students acquiring English gain proficiency with developing academic language skills.

TEACH IT!

To provide time to think and process

I. Encourage students to read a passage, then you discuss and model the comprehension strategy you want students to try out.

2. Give students time to think about the strategy in relation to what they are reading.

3. Encourage talking with a shoulder partner.

4. Invite students to write down their thinking to record their work with the comprehension strategy.

General Guidelines for Teaching a Strategy

1. Discuss the strategy.

2. Model the strategy using a chart of graphic organizer as a visual.

3. Practice the strategy—have students try the strategy out while reading.

4. Talk about the strategy—have students articulate with a partner what they were thinking and trying when using the strategy with text. Provide sentence frames as needed to support conversation.

5. Discuss students' thinking with the whole group at the table giving plenty of think time and support for students to talk.

6. Write about the strategy using sticky notes or journals to record thinking, and use graphic organizers to make the thinking process relate to the strategy visual. Provide response frames as needed to support writing about the conversation.

TEACHING COMPREHENSION BEFORE, DURING, AND AFTER READING

Comprehension instruction needs to be flexible and fluid. If you teach comprehension strategies in a mechanical way, you may be covering the objective of your lesson and teaching a comprehension strategy (check that off the list), but you will not be building in the flexibility that makes the instruction powerful. Students need time to think and talk about a text before they read, while they are reading, and after they read. Revisiting a text and discussing the text can help multilingual learners have clarity about the meaning of the text but also provide an opportunity for them to take their comprehension beyond a recall and restate level. They can work on constructing meaning using their own ideas and experiences. Comprehension instruction is a means to an end; it is not the end itself (Baker & Scher, 2002; Wilkenson & Son, 2011).

BEFORE-READING ACTIVITIES

Multilingual learners need the opportunity to engage what they know about topics and further develop their knowledge about topics and ideas before reading. Helping students make connections based on their varied backgrounds and experiences will increase student engagement and student understanding of the text. The prereading activities are like whetting the appetite before a meal. They get the readers ready for what they are going to be reading by generating interest. Don't make this mundane and perfunctory. Discuss ideas with gusto and talk up texts to get students excited about reading.

There are a few specific actions you can take to ramp up student interest and readiness to dive into texts. These actions include the following:

- Linking students' background knowledge and experiences with the topic or ideas presented in the text

- Preteaching vocabulary and concepts

- Setting a purpose for reading

- Reviewing text features

These activities prepare students to focus on what the text means and not just on decoding the words (Vaughn et al., 2007).

Linking Background Knowledge and Experiences

To link reading to what students already know means that they are going to need to talk and share stories (when relevant) (Gibbons, 2009). Personal narratives are powerful in engaging students and honoring what they know and who they are. You can build shared knowledge on a topic based on story sharing or thinking sharing. This act honors students' backgrounds and acknowledges that they have a lot to contribute.

TEACH IT!

1. Begin by introducing the topic of the text and then launch into some discussion.

2. Expand opportunities for students, purposefully and gently, to share what they know about the topic. Sometimes several students will have first-hand or second-hand knowledge of the topic and will have a story to share.

3. Check with the student first to make sure what they have to share is actually on topic and then give them time and space to share their story.

4. When they are done sharing, don't just move on; slow down and ask the other students what they are thinking now. How do they relate to the topic or the story the student(s) shared?

5. Preparing students to read is not about rushing through the preemptive steps to reading. It is about slowing down to ensure student comprehension.

Preteaching Vocabulary and Concepts

Don't slog through a long list of words before students start reading. Select two or three of the most important words to aid comprehension that students need to know before they start reading. Take a deep dive with these words.

TEACH IT!

1. Preview the word by pointing out where it is in the text.

2. Read the sentences around the word and make a prediction about what the word might mean.

3. Discuss the word meaning and the concept the word represents.

4. Don't worry about giving a dictionary definition, as it often has little meaning for students. Instead discuss the word and show pictures online or a short video clip on YouTube to illustrate the word.

5. After digging into the word's meaning, see if the students can define the word for themselves (Akhavan, 2009).

There will be more words that the students need to know than the two to three that you preteach, so stop and discuss words during the reading or go back and revisit the words after the reading. To do this, focus on the word's concept. What overall does it mean? Check out how the word is used in a sentence. Focus on students coming up with their own ideas about the word's meaning. If you need to, model using reference material to find the word meaning, but don't focus on dry definitions; spice up the learning of the word's meaning through discussion, prediction, and analysis.

Setting a Purpose for Reading

If you ask students why they are going to read something, they often answer with "I dunno, the teacher told me to read it." This is the starting point for helping students set a purpose for reading. You need to plan for students to read based on topics and ideas they are interested in. Don't just choose a text because it is next in your reading program. Ask your students about what they are interested in or note when they get excited about a topic you are discussing in class. Focus on bringing in texts on those topics.

Students often dive into reading without thinking why they are reading a text beyond the fact that it was assigned.

TEACH IT!

You can motivate students to read by

- Talking about the topic of text

- Providing context

- Juxtaposing ideas together (like how Americans love products packaged in plastic, but our landfills are filling up)

- Talk about the text topic, big idea, or highlight a main character

- Perhaps the biggest reason to read is to find out more . . . more about what happens to the characters, more about a topic that is exciting or interesting, or more about something that is happening in the world or how an author thinks and feels

- Discuss with students what they might want to find out and then set them up to read

Reviewing Text Features

When students survey a text before they start reading, they have an idea of what is going on in the text and what they might need to pay attention to. I find myself doing this when I am reading fiction or nonfiction. I might be checking the length of a chapter to make sure I am tracking along or looking at text features to help me understand the topic of the text.

Having students review text features before reading helps them and puts their mind around what they are going to read and focuses their attention on the topic (Akhavan, 2014). They are doing an appraisal of what they are going to read, as a way of settling in and getting ready.

TEACH IT!

Students can do the following to survey the text:

- Check chapter length and title of chapter

- Notice pictures in the text and what they depict

- Look at headings and predict what that section of a text might be about

- Analyze text boxes, graphs, statistics, or other features that provide information and clues to what the text might be about

Just having students go through looking at the text is not enough. The key is to talk about what they are seeing and thinking. Guide the students to come up with some broad ideas about the text before they start reading (Akhavan, 2014).

During-Reading Activities

While reading, students need to focus on decoding the words and thinking about what the text means. The more fluent a reader is, the easier time she will have with comprehending the text (Rasinski, 2010). As readers are able to simultaneously process text and understand and reflect on the features of the text by reading with prosody, students are likely to have greater comprehension (Rasinski et al., 2011).

Fluency is not the only factor in reading comprehension; language development is the foundation for reading comprehension (Rasinski & Young, 2014). I discuss oral language development in Chapter 5.

While students are reading text, we need to be there to support and coach them through what they are reading to ensure understanding.

TEACH IT!

These activities can include helping students:

- Monitor their reading

- Make connections while reading

- Ask questions while reading

- Chunking text

- Paraphrasing what the text says

- Getting the gist of the main idea

- Stopping to notice difficult vocabulary words or phrases

Comprehension Monitoring

Monitoring comprehension is more of a habit or skill than a strategy to teach. Set students up for success by getting them used to taking specific actions while reading in order to monitor that they understand what they are reading. There are a variety of strategies that you can teach students to practice. Once students practice these strategies, they will hopefully own these strategies for themselves and the strategies will become automatic skills that they apply when reading. In essence, comprehension monitoring is a self-regulatory skill (Gonzalez, 2007).

Students are often not aware of their own comprehending when they read. They are on automatic pilot, and they don't think or reflect on what is working for them and where things are breaking down (Harvey & Goudvis, 2013; Pitts, 1983). Comprehension monitoring includes self-questioning. Help students monitor their own comprehension by stopping from time to time and asking themselves a few questions.

TEACH IT!

Model and guide students to ask themselves questions such as the following:

- Do I get what I just read?

- Does what I read make sense?

- Do I know the meaning of the words that seem important?

- How can I figure out the meaning of the words?

- Do the sentences make sense?

- How does the information in this text fit with what I already know?

- How does what is happening in the story fit with things I know about?

Making Connections While Reading

There have been recent calls to move beyond personal connections when working with students on comprehension. For instance, Serafini (2014) noted that new expectations in reading call for a shift away from students making personal connections to text and instead focusing on interpreting the language and structure of the text. It is true that students do need to interpret language and think of text structure to guide their comprehension; however, students who are multilingual learners need a place to "hook" their thinking as they add vocabulary and understanding of language structures to their knowledge base. While making connections to text is not an end goal for reading comprehension, it is a helpful place to start.

Having students make connections to text based on what they know about the world is a way of activating students background knowledge. You can help them make connections to the text and articulate these connections in order to make sense of what they are reading.

CONNECTIONS

When good readers read, they make connections between their own life experiences and knowledge and what is happening in the text. They will also make connections between the experiences, events, information, and phenomena that they have background knowledge in and the text; when reading texts with similar topics and themes or plots, they make connections between texts. Known as text-to-self, text-to-text, and text-to-world connections, the power of text connections for multilingual language learners cannot be overlooked. When students make text-to-text connections, they are specifically looking at the vocabulary and language structures of the text to draw meaning between texts.

Text Connections for Emerging and Developing Students

Text connections are important. Since they still don't know the meaning of all vocabulary they are reading and they may not understand the nuances of theme or character development in fiction or the content points and topic in nonfiction, students at the emerging and developing phases of proficiency in English need to focus their comprehension on the most basic level of comprehension: text-to-self connections. Of course, they need to grow beyond using only this comprehension strategy fairly rapidly, but it is a good place to start.

TEACH IT!

- Asking "How can you relate what you read to something you already know?" is powerful. Since the thinking is focused on the personal connection to text, students can think of how what they already know relates to the text.

- Providing an array of books for students that reflect their backgrounds, experiences, and interests reinforces students being able to make text-to-self connections.

Asking Questions While Reading

Teachers are often in the driver's seat at the reading table and ask the majority of the questions to ensure students are comprehending what they are reading; however, this does not build self-regulation of reading comprehension (Pressley, 2006). To help readers monitor their own comprehension and guide their own thinking about what they are reading, they need to ask questions about the text themselves (James & Carter, 2007; Joseph & Ross, 2017). Multilingual students often rely on us to ask the questions, but we need to engage students to ask the questions themselves.

- Students can start by asking basic questions like *who, what, when,* and *where* about the text they are reading, and then, most importantly, they can dive into the text to explicitly find the answers.

- When students answer without referencing the text, encourage them to find the place in the text that backs up their thinking.

- As students grow in their ability to ask questions and find the answers of questions themselves, they can stretch into asking *why* and *how* questions. Why and how questions are not always answered explicitly in the text, and students may need to find more than one place in a book or text to answer their questions.

- Why and how questions lead students to make inferences about characters' thoughts and feelings based on actions or on why the details in an informational text lead to an overall understanding of a topic or issue (Mathes et al., 2007; Pressley & Wharton-McDonald, 1997). How and why questions develop students' skills at inferring the answers about what happened or how someone did something that may not be explicitly written out, and students will have to look at different parts of the text and put their ideas together to make an inference.

To help multilingual learners see the answers in the text or find parts of the text that help them make an inference, it can be helpful to give them a sticky note to place under the line of text that helps with the answer. If they are using a copied text or electronic text, they can highlight the part of the text and even the part of the sentence that help them answer explicitly. By focusing attention on the specific parts of the text or the sentence, they don't have to process the entire text at once and can just focus on the language and structures of the language that they are reading and working through (Carnine et al., 1997).

TEACH IT!

To guide students to ask questions of text

- Practice with *who, what, when,* and *where* questions first. These are green-level questions, as students' thinking can be fast and quick, referring back to the text to explicitly answer their own questions.

- Once students can identify answers to who, what, when, and where questions, encourage them to ask *why* and *how* questions. These are yellow-level questions. Students need to slow down and consider the parts of the text that help them answer.

- Students can continue asking inferential questions and come up with the most important question of all—they can write down their question and then write the answer and explain what parts of the text helped them answer the question.

Sentence Starters for Answering the Most Important Question

Help students kick-start their thinking to identify the most important point to question:

- What question helped you get to the biggest idea about the text?

- What seems to be the author's important points? What would you ask the author?

- What information is repeated or explained in detail? What questions do you have about this information?

Most **IMPORTANT** Question . . .

_____

_____

_____

Figure it out! Write the answer to the most important question below.

_____

_____

_____

_____

_____

online resources

As students become more practiced in asking questions that help them focus on making meaning from the text, they can begin working on answering the questions that they are asking or that you are asking (Ness, 2016). Remember that multilingual learners learn best through interactive instruction with an element of direct instruction (Genesee et al., 2005).

TEACH IT!

- Encourage students to talk with you about the strategies you are using after you do a model using a strategy.

- The more discussion they are involved in about a strategy, the better they will understand how to use the strategy.

- Discussion develops their understanding of text.

- To stay focused on interactive instruction, you can focus on talking through the answers to questions and help students find text evidence to back up their answers (Pearson & Johnson, 1978).

How to Ask Deep Questions

Too often we focus on asking students questions focused on skills at the word or sentence level rather than helping them think deeply about text (Degener & Berne, 2016). Students need to understand the text at the word and sentence level, but the questions we ask need to help them understand the text and monitor their own understanding while building and developing their knowledge of what they are reading and develop background knowledge. Questions at the deeper level encourage the students to understand how the text's meaning fits in with his or her understanding of the world (Degener & Berne, 2016).

Text-Explicit Questions

One type of question that students will be answering is text-explicit questions. These are the answers to the green questions: *who, what, when,* and *where.* Students will be able to find the answer directly in the text. I have discussed these types of questions in the preceding section. Green questions are literal questions, and students will be able to find the answers *right in* the text without having to interpret information in the text to answer.

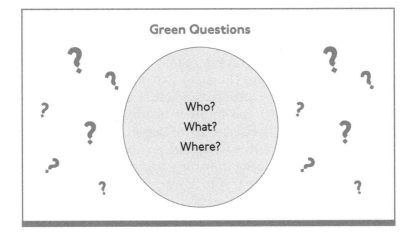

Text-Implicit Questions

Text-implicit questions lead students to interpret text in order to answer. Text-implicit questions include making inferences. These types of questions include the questions below. Text-implicit questions make students slow down and think carefully about the answers to the questions. They may have to refer to several different parts of the text or different sentences in more than one place in the text to answer (Spear-Swirling & Cheessman, 2012).

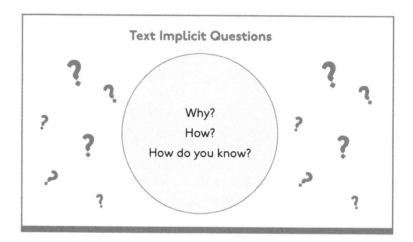

Script-Implicit Questions

Pearson and Johnson (1978) once said that the process of comprehension is "building bridges between the new and the unknown" (p. 24). This bridge that students build is their background knowledge. There are also questions where students have to apply their background knowledge in addition to what the text says in order to answer the questions (Spear-Swerling & Cheessman, 2015; Degener & Berne, 2016). Sometimes students either ignore the text completely and try to answer questions using only their background knowledge, or they only rely on the text to answer, not referring to what they already know and how what the text says enhances their knowledge (Raphael, 1982). When students apply their background knowledge to a question while considering what the text says, they synthesize information to come up with a new understanding. These are questions that have students apply their knowledge in order to answer (Raphael & Au, 2005). Questions to encourage students to apply their knowledge and reference the text are blue questions. These are initiating questions to encourage thinking and conversation about text (Beck & McKeown, 2006).

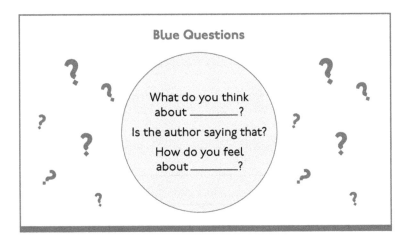

QUESTIONS TO ENCOURAGE STUDENTS TO APPLY THEIR KNOWLEDGE AND CHECK THE TEXT

What is the author trying to say here?

How do you know?

What is the author talking about?

What does it mean?

How does all of this information fit together?

How do the character actions relate to the outcomes?

Why do you think the author tells us this now?

Given what the author has said, what do you think now?

Adapted from Beck and McKeown (2006).

Questioning

Date: _____

Title: _____

Author: _____

Genre: _____

Questions **BEFORE** reading:

_____

_____

Questions **DURING** reading:

_____

_____

Questions **AFTER** reading:

_____

_____

Were you able to answer any of your questions?

_____

_____

What did you use to answer your questions?

_____

_____

_____

_____

Chunk and Paraphrase

Teaching students help themselves while reading lifts students up so that they can control their reading process. One skill that I have found to work is Stop, Think, Say. The strategy Stop, Think, Say, or STS for short, is developed from research by Hoff (2013), who studied what instructions in class support multilingual students to be most successful. Hoff noted that this needs to include more student talk and less teacher talk.

Stop, Think, Say is a relatively easy strategy. To practice Stop, Think, Say, students read a chunk of text and then they stop reading, pause for a moment, and think about what the text said. Then, in their head, to a partner or maybe even writing down a jot, students say what the text said in their own words, paraphrasing. I have had teachers ask me if it is important if students look at the text to reread to double-check meaning. I answer, "Of course!" Encourage students to reread to check their comprehension. Stop, Think, Say is not about students working from memory (thus closing the book or turning a page so they cannot look at it to support themselves in thinking) but encouraging students to focus on their comprehension, using the book to remember and guide. The book acts as a scaffold for multilingual students to monitor their own comprehension. It also helps them to realize that the text itself is a scaffold when they go back and reread.

TEACH IT!

Think about guiding students in Stop, Think, Say. Notice the following:

- What do they remember?
- What do they need to double-check in the chunk of text they read?
- What do they think the text is saying?

AFTER-READING ACTIVITIES

Much of what I recommend as after-reading strategies include students discussing text and writing about text.

Visualizing

Visualizing is the comprehension strategy that my research has shown to be the least used strategy by students as they get older (Akhavan, 2019). I am not sure why this is—perhaps students don't realize that reading should result in them "seeing" action and ideas. Visualizing is a helpful strategy for multilingual students; while they might not always have the language proficiency to express their thinking about their reading, they can certainly concretely create pictures in their minds about what they are reading, even if the pictures don't contain all the details that the text provides.

- The first step to visualization is a close examination of what the text is saying. Students would look at the words in the sentence to make sure they understand the words.

- The second step is to create a picture in the mind's eye based on what the sentences are saying. Students can work on the meaning of the sentences together.

Seeing pictures or diagrams in their mind of what the text is saying can help multilingual students focus on both the words being used in the text and what the words are saying. Students may need you to prompt their thinking. "Make a picture in your mind" or "Make a movie in your mind" can help students "see" what they are reading in live action or in still pictures. Provide a thinking frame and encourage students to use the thinking frame to write after they stop and visualize.

TEACH IT!

Frames that support visualization include the following:

- Make a picture in your mind based on the words in the story/text.
- Make a movie in your mind.
- What do you see?
- What is happening?
- What do you think will happen next?

Note how the preceding writing frames prompt students to share what they see. You could talk through the writing frame first; students could then write or draw with you, and you could continue with the discussion, students using their notes to help them talk.

Visualization

Date: _____

Title: _____

Author: _____

Genre: _____

What exactly does the book say? _____

_____

_____

_____

What does my mind <u>see?</u>

My thinking about my visualization: _____

_____

_____

_____

_____

Retelling and Summarizing

Before students can summarize text, they need to be able to retell. Retelling orally or in writing significantly improves students' comprehension of what they are reading (Koskinen et al., 1988). Retelling is a skill that spirals into summarization (Stoutz, 2011). For multilingual learners, their ability to retell is going to depend on their ability to understand the text in English and also their level of English language acquisition (Lucero, 2018). They may understand the concepts of what they are reading but not have sufficient vocabulary in English in order to express themselves through retelling (Lucero, 2018).

TEACH IT!

Try the following approaches to support retelling and summarizing:

- Students who understand the story or text but need to express their retelling in their heritage language should be encouraged to do so.

- Students who are at the **emerging** level of language acquisition can retell using pictures and graphics.

- As students acquire more language, they may begin by retelling in short sentences that don't give numerous details.

- Students will grow in their ability to add detail to their retellings once they acquire more language and can express themselves.

It can be very helpful for multilingual learners to use graphic organizers to help them retell. The diagrams and pictures that the students can put together can help them structure the information they want to share and indicate the relationships amongst the information (Kim et al., 2004; Phantharakphong & Pothitha, 2014).

Students can create character maps as part of a retell, sequence events in a story or text, or depict relationships regarding topics in an informational text. A simple graphic organizer to use is a circle for retelling (see page 199). You can also model how to create a circle retell with different relationships between events or information in a story to help a student retell (see picture on page 199).

Source: The Big Book of Literacy Tasks, Grades K–8, Akhavan (2018).

Story Structure

Name: _____   Date: _____

Title: _____

_____

Author: _____

Genre:

Characters:

Setting:

Problem:

Solution:

When students are reading stories, they can use story structure to help them retell.

- Students can retell by sharing the characters, setting, problem, action, and resolution of the problem.

- Story maps are helpful graphic organizers to guide students through their retelling of a story. Using a story map, students will be able to analyze the parts of a story and then share their learnings orally or in writing.

- Five-finger retelling (Stahl, 2004) is also helpful because students can use their hand to help them remember each part of the text.

- You can also use the mnemonic STORE to help students retell each part of a story (Bos, 1989). As students write out their retellings, it is helpful to provide sentence starters or paragraph frames to guide their thinking.

Story Structure

Name: _____ Date: _____

Today I read _____ by _____ . It is a nonfiction book.

I know this because I found _____ , _____ , and

_____ . Form this book I learned _____

_____

_____

_____

_____

_____

_____

_____

_____

_____

_____ .

Name: _____ Date: _____

BEFORE READING: ASK, THINK, JOT

STEP 1: Ask yourself:

"Do I understand why I am reading this section?"

If you answered YES: Write the purpose below.

If you answered NO: Skim the section again, check your notes, and give it a try.

STEP 2: Skim the headings, bold words, and graphics.

Ask yourself: *"What is the section or page about?"* and *"What details support the main idea?"*

(Write your jots here)

STEP 3: Summarize what you read.

(Write your summary here)

Source: The Nonfiction Now Lesson Bank, Grades 4–8, Akhavan (2014), p. 291.

Determining Importance

Multilingual students will need guidance in learning how to determine what is important in what they are reading. If students are not grasping what the text is saying, they may not be able to determine what is important to focus on or remember (Rapp et al., 2007). Students may think that everything in the text is equally important. When this happens and they are highlighting the text, everything in the text might be pink, yellow, or blue.

When students are working with informational text, it is important for them to grasp what is important so that they can learn the information in the text as well as enjoy what they are reading! The key is helping students connect the information to what they are interested in, what they want to know, or make links to what they already know and enhance their learning.

One way of helping English language learners determine important points on their own is to help them unlock the text features so that they can see the meaning that the text features provide (Bluestein, 2010). There are internal and external text features (Moss, 2005).

TEACH IT!

External text features to teach include the following:

- The table of contents
- Index
- Bold words
- Other features that are evident

Internal text features to teach include the following:

- How the text is put together, as in the organization of the text
- The purpose of the text also provides organization to the text
- Depending on what the author intended to convey, he or she will organize the text in order to convey that meaning

Narrative nonfiction texts like biographies are a good place to start for multilingual learners. The text is structured like a story, and that is familiar to readers. The story text structure can help them pull out the ideas of what is important to remember (Bluestein, 2010). Students can focus on the setting that is discussed in the biography, the events in the life of the person focused on, and the actions that the person took in order to be well known. They can also consider how the person's character is discussed. Once students have some practice with identifying important points in a nonfiction text that follows a story structure, they can use their successes to focus on determining important points in other types of nonfiction text.

Main Idea, Details

Students can work to identify the main idea and details by focusing closely on what the text says (Akhavan, 2019). Students can also read to get the gist of the section of text they are working on. When they read to get the gist, they are reading not to understand every detail that may be important but rather to grasp the main idea and a couple of details that support the main idea. In getting the gist, they are reading to see what the text is mainly about (Akhavan, 2014).

Get the Gist

Name: _____ Date: _____

Title of Text: _____

Page	Notes From Text (use bullets)	What I Think This Means

Here's the Gist of the Text

Source: The Nonfiction Now Lesson Bank, Grades 4–8, Akhavan (2014), p. 191.

TEACH IT!

Invite students to

- Read a section of text and then identify three main points
- Look for repeating words and phrases
- Look for topic sentences that are backed up with sentences providing detail on the topic

In this section on comprehension, you have what you need to scaffold multilingual students' understanding of texts. Probably the most important thing I can say to conclude is to remember, less is more. That is, during your twenty minutes together, teach just a couple of strategies so that students have time to think, try them, and talk about their understandings.

Concluding Thoughts

Teaching multilingual children to read is never just about decoding or fluency or stamina—or any of the myriad skills involved in literacy. The endeavor is so much bigger, so much more life-affirming than that. When you gather students at the reading table and open them to the experiences described in this book, you are teaching them to understand the world. To read, to write, to think, to reflect, to debate, to change their minds, to walk in another's footsteps, to invent, and to put their stamp on this earth.

As I said at the outset, I am with you in this wonderful, important work. I encourage you to contact me with questions or insights: Twitter@nancyakhavan.

Appendix

1. Elkonin Boxes

2. Phonics Instructional Goals

3. Spelling Inventory Score Sheet

4. "The Most Important Words for Second Language Learners of English" from the New General Service List Project

5. Entering Lesson Sequence

6. Emerging Lesson Sequence

7. Developing Lesson Sequence

8. Expanding Lesson Sequence

9. Bridging Level Sequence

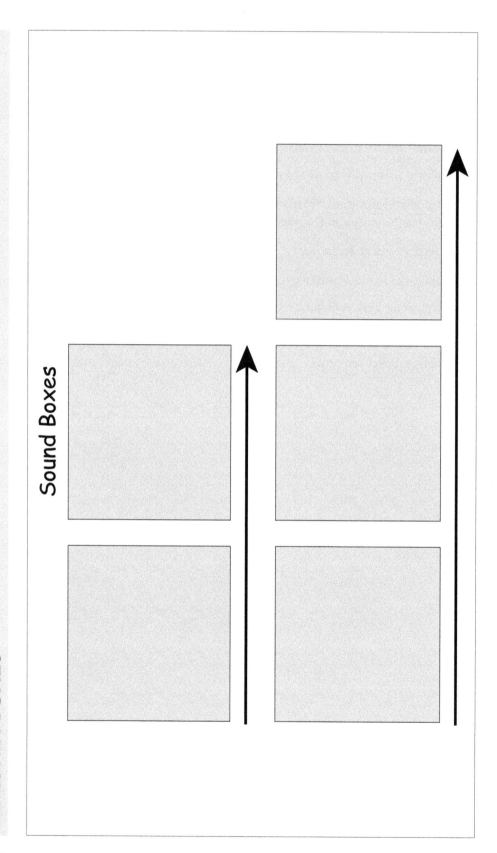

Sound Boxes

Sound Boxes

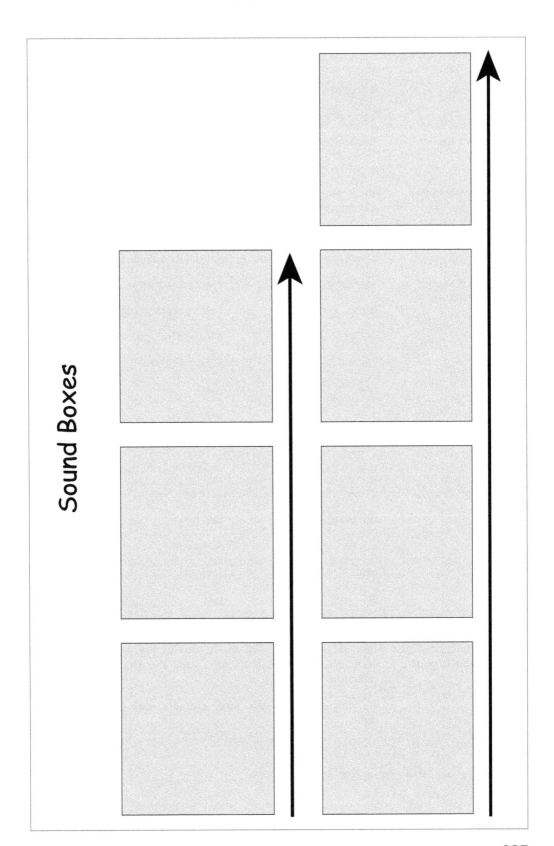

PHONICS INSTRUCTIONAL GOALS

Letter names	Introduce in an order to maximize making words a m t s i f d r o g l h u c b n k v e w j p y x q z	
Consonant sounds	Introduce in an order to maximize making words m t s f d r g l h c b n k v w j p x q z	
Consonant blends	bl, cl, fl, gl, pl, sl, br, cr, dr, fr, gr, pr, tr, sc, sk, sm, sn, sp, st, sw, tw, scr, shr, spl, spr, str, thr	
Diagraphs & tigraphs	Ch, sh, ng, ph, th, wh, tch, dge	
Vowel sounds	Short and long sounds represented by a single letter	
Long vowel sounds with alternative spelling	ai, ay, a-e	maid, play, made
	ee, ea, e-e, ei, y	bee, beneath, hungry
	ie, igh, y, i-e	pie, light, my, pike
	ow, oe, o-e	slow, toe, dote
	u-e	use
Short vowel sounds with alternative spelling	e, ea	bed, deadi
	i, y	tip, myth
	u, o	mud, come, mother
Dipthongs	oi, oy	oil, boy
	ou, ow	out, how
	eu, ew	eureka, few
	ure	sure
	ai	pair
R-controlled vowels	ar, er, ir, or, ur	
Orthographic similarity, intrasyllable linguistic rime	-an, -ap, -at, -aw, -ay, -in, -ip, -it, -op, -ot, -ug, -ack, -ail-, -ain, -ake, -ale, -all, -ame, -amp, -ank, -ash, -ate, -eat, -ell, -est, -ice, -ick, -ide, -ill, -ine, -ing, -ink-, -ock, -oke, -old, -ore, -uck, -ump, -unk, -ight	
Morphemes	Prefixes, suffixes	

Adapted from Bald, 2007; Tolman, 2005; Westwood, 2001.

SPELLING INVENTORY

Primary Spelling Inventory

(adapted from Francine Johnston, July 1998)

Purpose of Primary Spelling Inventory

To assess the word knowledge students have to bring to the tasks of reading and spelling.

Students are not to study these words. Studying the words would invalidate the purpose of the inventory, which is to find out what they truly know about how words work.

Setting

This assessment can be administered to small groups (recommended in K–1) or the whole class.

Materials

Sentences for words

Individual score sheet

Class composite sheet

Blank paper for students

Guidelines for Administration

Call out the word and use it in a sentence (just as you would for any spelling test).

Score each student's assessment and record results on the individual score sheet.

Record class results on the class composite.

The words are ordered in terms of their relative difficulty for children in grades K–5. For this reason, you only need to administer the words that your students are likely to master during the year. Following you will find the recommended word count per grade level:

Kindergarten: The first five to eight words

First grade: At least the first fifteen words

Second and third grade: The entire list

For those students who are spelling most words correctly in kindergarten and first grade, you may call out additional words.

Scoring

Check off or highlight the features for each word that are spelled according to the descriptors at the top.

Assign 1 point for each feature (some words are scored for some features and not others).

Add an additional point in the "Word Correct" column for entire words that are spelled correctly.

Total the number of points **across each word and under each feature**.

Review the feature columns in order to determine the individual needs of your students.

If a student does not receive any points for a particular feature, that feature is beyond their instructional level and the earlier features should be addressed first.

Sentences for Administration Word	Sentence	Word
1. fan	I could use a **fan** on a hot day.	fan
2. pet	I have a **pet** cat who likes to play.	pet
3. dig	He will **dig** a hole in the sand.	dig
4. rob	A raccoon will **rob** a bird's nest for eggs.	rob
5. hope	I **hope** you will do well on the test.	hope
6. wait	You will need to **wait** for the letter.	wait
7. gum	I stepped in some bubble **gum**.	gum
8. sled	The dog **sled** was pulled by huskies.	sled

Sentences for Administration Word	Sentence	Word
You may stop here in kindergarten, unless a student has spelled five words correctly.		
9. stick	I used a **stick** to poke in the hole.	stick
10. shine	He rubbed the coin to make it **shine**.	shine
11. dream	I had a funny **dream** last night.	dream
12. blade	The **blade** of the knife was very sharp.	blade
13. coach	The **coach** called the team off the field.	coach
14. fright	She was a **fright** in her costume.	fright
15. chewing	Don't talk until you finish **chewing** your food.	chewing
You may stop here in first grade unless a student has spelled ten words correctly.		
16. crawl	You will get dirty if you **crawl** under the bed.	crawl
17. wishes	In fairy tales, **wishes** often come true.	wishes
18. thorn	The **thorn** from the rosebush stuck me.	thorn
19. shouted	They **shouted** at the barking dog.	shouted
20. spoil	The food will **spoil** if it sits out too long.	spoil
21. growl	The dog will **growl** if you bother him.	growl
22. third	I was the **third** person in line.	third
23. camped	We **camped** down by the river last weekend.	camped
24. tries	He **tries** hard every day to finish his work.	tries
25. clapping	The audience was **clapping** after the program.	clapping
26. riding	They are **riding** their bikes to the park today.	riding

SPELLING INVENTORY SCORE SHEET

Using the key on page 124 of Chapter 6, check off the type of spelling pattern the child is representing in the words they have written on the spelling test.

Name _____   Date _____

Target Word	Precommunicative	Prephonetic	Phonetic	Transitional Patterns	Transitional Syllable	Derivational Meaning	Correct Spelling
fan							
pet							
dig							
rob							
hope							
wait							
gum							
sled							
stick							
shine							
dream							

Target Word	Precommunicative	Prephonetic	Phonetic	Transitional Patterns	Transitional Syllable	Derivational Meaning	Correct Spelling
blade							
coach							
fright							
chewing							
crawl							
wishes							
thorn							
shouted							
spoil							
growl							
third							
camped							
tries							
clapping							
riding							

"THE MOST IMPORTANT WORDS FOR SECOND LANGUAGE LEARNERS OF ENGLISH" FROM THE NEW GENERAL SERVICE LIST PROJECT

http://www.newgeneralservicelist.org/ngsls/

ENTERING LESSON SEQUENCE

Day 1

Step 1: Work with sounds

Step 2: Work with letters

Step 3: Work with everyday vocabulary

Day 2

Step 1: Work with sounds

Step 2: Work with letters

Step 3: Read poems and sing songs

Day 3

Step 1: Work with sounds

Step 2: Work with letters

Step 3: Read a predictable story

Step 4: Shared writing

Work With Sounds

Pictures representing sounds

Phoneme isolation

Blending sounds

Phoneme substitution

Adding and deleting sounds

Substituting sounds

Working With Letters

Letter/Sound matching

Letter name identification

Blending

Spelling CVC words

Working With Everyday Vocabulary

Labeling objects in classroom

Working with small items and naming/labeling

Practicing simple phrases

Total physical response (TPR)

Work With Poems, Songs, Books

Singing songs

Reciting poetry using visual charts with pictures

Previewing books

Discussing illustrations

Acting out songs, poems, simple stories

Shared Writing

Shared or interactive writing experience

○ EMERGING LESSON SEQUENCE

Day 1

Step 1: Work with sounds

Step 2: Work with sight words

Step 3: Shared reading of predictable text

Day 2

Step 1: Work with sounds—focus on decoding

Step 2: Share reading decodable text

Step 3: Share reading from poem or choral reading/singing from a songbook, making sure to discuss the text to build oral language

Day 3

Step 1: Work with sounds—focus on writing words

Step 2: Work on vocabulary you will use in the sentences

Step 3: Dictate sentences using the vocabulary words

Step 4: Draw a picture and write a sentence about the story from Day 1 or Day 2 using a sentence frame

---

Work With Sounds	**Working With Sight Words**
Blending sounds	Decode word
Phoneme substitution	Play games with words
Adding and deleting sounds	Write words
Substituting sounds	Create word lists
	Work on fluent reading of words

Working With Vocabulary	**Shared Reading**
Discuss book pictures	Read and sing songs together
Practice simple phrases	Reciting poetry using visual charts
Total Physical Response (TPR) Create word banks	Read books together with teacher reading aloud
Use sentence frames	

Develop Oral Language	**Guided Writing**
Encourage speaking in simple phrases	Model writing sentences
Asking yes/no questions	Compose sentences together
Ask for ideas	Guide students to write words

DEVELOPING LESSON SEQUENCE

Day 1

Step 1: Sight word review

Step 2: Teach decoding skills or comprehension strategy

Step 3: Introduce new book

Step 4: Read

Step 5: Discuss

Day 2

Step 1: Discuss book/review key vocabulary

Step 2: Read book again

Step 3: Guided writing

Working With Sight Words

Decode word

Dictate words

Say it, Stretch it, Write it

Create word lists

Work on fluent reading of words

Working With Vocabulary

Discuss book pictures

Practice simple phrases

Create word banks

Use sentence frames

Guided Writing

Think, plan, write

Guide students to write sentences between three and ten words

Focus on spelling

Teaching Point

Word solving—decoding

Word solving for meaning—discuss

Retelling

Main idea and details

Character, plot, setting

○ EXPANDING LESSON SEQUENCE

Day 1

Step 1: Introduce and preview text

Step 2: Vocabulary preteach

Step 3: Read

Step 4: Discuss comprehension

Step 5: Write

Step 6: Assign independent reading

Day 2

Step 1: Discuss for comprehension

Step 2: Teach unknown vocabulary

Step 3: Teach comprehension strategy

Step 4: Practice comprehension strategy

Step 5: Write in reading journal

Day 3

Step 1: Discuss reading

Step 2: Teach unknown vocabulary

Step 3: Shared writing about text

Step 4: Discuss text

Working With Vocabulary

Discuss sentences around the word

Practice use in sentences and phrases

Create word banks

Use sentence frames

Write About Reading

Write focusing on a comprehension strategy

Comprehension Strategies

Predict

Ask and answer questions

Summarize main idea and details

Infer, using text structures and text features

Visualize

Compare and contrast

BRIDGING LESSON SEQUENCE

Day 1

Step 1: Set purpose for reading

Step 2: Introduce book

Step 3: Teach comprehension strategy

Step 4: Read

Step 5: Discuss

Step 6: Write about their reading

Working With Vocabulary

Discuss sentences around the word

Practice use in sentences and phrases

Create word banks

Use sentence frames

Write About Reading

Write focusing on a comprehension strategy

Comprehension Strategies

Predict

Ask and answer questions

Summarize main idea and details

Infer using text structures and text features

Visualize

Compare and contrast

Reading Purpose

Explore topics

Understand theme and human experience

Connect ideas together

Answer questions

Make meaning from text

References

Akhavan, N. L. (2006). *Help! My kids don't all speak English: How to set up a language workshop in your linguistically diverse classroom.* Heinemann.

Akhavan, N. (2007). *Accelerated vocabulary instruction: Strategies for closing the achievement gap for all students.* Scholastic.

Akhavan, N. L. (2009). *Teaching writing in a Title I school.* Heinemann.

Akhavan, N. L. (2014). *The nonfiction now lesson bank, grades 4–8: Strategies and routines for higher-level comprehension in the content areas.* Corwin.

Akhavan, N. L. (2019). *At the reading table with striving readers: Achieving equity by scaffolding skills and strategies.* Benchmark Education.

Akhavan, N., & Walsh, N. (2020). Cognitive apprenticeship learning approach in K–8 writing instruction: A case study. *Journal of Education and Learning, 9*(3), 123. https://doi.org/10.5539/jel.v9n3p123

Anderson, R. C., & Nagy, W. E. (1992). The vocabulary conundrum. *American Educator: The Professional Journal of the American Federation of Teachers, 16*(4), 14–18.

Anderson, R. C., Wilson, P. T., & Fielding. L. G. (1988). Growth in reading and how children spend their time. *Reading Research Quarterly, 23*(3), 285–303.

Apel, K., & Henbest, V. S. (2016). Affix meaning knowledge in first through third grade students. *Language, Speech, and Hearing Services in Schools, 47*(2), 148–156.

Ariam, A. (2017). *Guided reading at the frustrational level.* [thesis]. Department of Educational Leadership, Fresno State.

August, D. (2003). Supporting the development of English literacy in English language learners: Key issues and promising practices (Reports-Descriptive No. 61).

Center for Research on the Education of Students Placed at Risk (CRESPAR), Johns Hopkins University.

August, D., Carlo, M., Dressler, C., & Snow, C. (2005). The critical role of vocabulary development for English language learners. *Learning Disabilities Research & Practice, 20*(1), 50–57.

Baker, L., & Scher, D. (2002). Beginning readers motivation for reading in relation to parental beliefs and home reading experiences. *Reading Psychology, 23*(4), 239–269.

Bald, J. (2007). *Using phonics to teach reading and spelling.* Sage.

Bao, D. (2014). *Understanding silence and reticence: Ways of participating in second language acquisition.* Bloomsbury.

Bates (2021). *Interactive writing.* Benchmark Education.

Bear, D. R., Helman, L., & Woessner, L. (2009). Word study assessment and instruction with English learners in a second grade classroom: Bending with students' growth. In J. Coppola & E. Primas (Eds.), *Teaching and learning in linguistically and culturally diverse classrooms: Bringing theory and research to practice* (pp. 11–40). International Reading Association.

Bear, D. R., & Smith, R. E. (2012). The literacy development of English learners: What do we know about each student's literacy development. In L. Helman (Ed.), *Literacy development with English learners: Research based instruction grades K–6* (pp. 87–116). Routledge.

Beck, I. L., & McKeown, M. G. (2006). *Improving comprehension with questioning the author: A fresh and expanded view of a powerful approach.* Scholastic.

Beck, I. L., McKeown, M. G., & Kucan, L. (2013). *Bringing words to life: Robust vocabulary instruction* (2nd ed.). Guilford Press.

Bermudez, A. B., & Prater, D. L. (1994). Examining the effects of gender and second language proficiency on Hispanic persuasive discourse. *Bilingual Research Journal, 18*(3), 47–62.

Bialik, K., Scheller, A., & Walker, K. (2018). 6 facts about English language learners in U.S. public schools. Pew Research Center. https://www.pewresearch.org/fact-tank/2018/10/25/6-facts-about-english-language-learners-in-u-s-public-schools/

Biemiller, A., & Slonim, N. (2001). Estimating root word vocabulary growth in normative and advantaged populations: Evidence for a common sequence of vocabulary acquisition. *Journal of Educational Psychology, 93*(3), 498–520.

Billings, E., & Walqui, A. (n.d.). *Dispelling the myth of "English Only": Understanding the importance of the first language in second language learning.* NYSED Office of bilingual and world languages. https://www.nysed.gov/common/nysed/files/dispelling_myth_rev-2.pdf

Birsh, R. B., & Carreker, S. (2018). *Multisensory teaching of basic language skills.* Brookes Publishing.

Blachowicz, C., & Fisher, P. J. (2002). *Teaching vocabulary in all classrooms.* Pearson.

Bland, J. (2013). *Children's literature and learner empowerment: Children and Teenagers in English language education.* Bloomsbury.

Blevins, W. (2017). *Teaching phonics and word study in the intermediate grades* (2nd ed.). Scholastic.

Blevins, W. (2020). *From phonics to reading, grades K–3.* Sadlier.

Blevins, W. (2021). *Choosing and using decodable text: Practical tips and strategies for enhancing phonics instruction.* Scholastic.

Bluestein, N. A. (2010). Unlocking text features for determining importance in expository text: A strategy for struggling readers. *The Reading Teacher, 63*(7), 597–600.

Bos, C. S., Anders, P. L., Filip, D., & Jaffe, L. E. (1989). The effects of an interactive instructional strategy for enhancing learning disabled students' reading comprehension and content area learning. *Journal of Learning Disabilities, 22,* 384–390.

Bowey, J. A. (2002). Reflections on onset-rime and phoneme sensitivity as predictors of beginning word reading. *Journal of Experimental Child Psychology, 82,* 29–40.

Brookes, D. B., & Jeong, A. (2006). Effects of pre-structuring discussion threads on group interaction and group performance in computer-supported collaborative argumentation. *Distance Education, 27*(3), 371–390.

Brown, J. I. (1947). Reading and vocabulary: 14 master words. In M. J. Herzberg (Ed.), *Word study* (pp. 1–4). G. & C. Merriam.

Browne, C., Culligan, B., & Phillips. J. (2013). New general service list project. http://www.newgeneralservicelist.org/

Brozo, W. G. (2002). *To be a boy, to be a reader.* International Reading Association.

Burns, M. K., & Sterling-Turner, H. E. (2010). Comparison of efficiency measures for academic interventions based on acquisition and maintenance. *Psychology in the Schools, 47*(2), 126–134.

Cain, K., & Oakhill, J. V. (1999). Inference making ability and its relation to comprehension failure in young children. *Reading and Writing: An Interdisciplinary Journal, 11*(5–6), 489–503.

Calderón, M. E., & Sinclair-Slakk, S. M. (2018). *Teaching reading to English learners, grades 6–12: A framework for improving achievement in the content areas* (2nd ed.). Corwin.

Calderón, M. E., & Soto, I. (2017). *Academic language mastery: Vocabulary in context.* Corwin.

Cameron, L. (2001). *Teaching languages to young learners.* Cambridge University Press.

Campos, M. M., Bhering, E. B., Espósito, Gimenes, N., Abuchaim, B., Valle, R., Unbehaum, S., & Carlos Chagas Foundation. (2011). The contribution of quality early childhood education and its impacts on the beginning of fundamental education. *Educação e Pesquisa, 37,* 15–33.

Carey, S. (1978). The child as word learner. Linguistic theory and psychological reality. In M. Halle, J. Bresnan, & G. A. Miller (Eds.), *Linguistic theory and psychological reality* (pp. 264–293). MIT Press.

Carlisle, J. (2010). Effects of instruction in morphological awareness on literacy achievement: An integrative review. *Reading Research Quarterly, 45*(4), 464–487.

Carlo, M. S., August, D., McLaughlin, B., Snow, C. E., Dressler, C., Lippman, D. N., Lively, T. J., & White, C. E. (2004). Closing the gap: Addressing the vocabulary needs of English language learners in bilingual and mainstream classrooms. *Reading Research Quarterly, 39*(2), 188–215.

Carnegie Council on Advancing Adolescent Literacy. (2010). *Time to act: An agenda for advancing adolescent literacy for college and career success.* Carnegie Corporation for New York.

Carnine, D., Silbert, J. & Kame'enui, E. J. (1997). *Direct instruction reading* (3rd ed.). Merrill.

Carrell, P. L. (1992). Awareness of text structure: Effects on recall. *Language Learning 42*(1), 1–20.

Catts, H. W., Adolf, S. M., & Weismer, S. E. (2006). Language deficits in poor comprehenders: A case for the simple view of reading. *Journal of Speech, Language, and Hearing Research, 49*(2), 278–293.

Cazden, C. B. (2001). *Classroom discourse: The language of teaching and learning* (2nd ed.). Heinemann.

Cazden, C. B. (2017). *Communicative competence, classroom interaction, and educational equity: The selected works of Courtney B. Cazden.* Routledge.

Cervetii, G. N., & Hiebert, E. H. (2015). The sixth pillar of reading instruction: Knowledge development. *The Reading Teacher, 68*(7), 548–551.

Chacón-Beltrán, R., Abello-Contesse, C., & del Mar Torreblanca-López, M. (2010). *Insights into non-native vocabulary teaching and learning.* Channel View Publications.

Chall, J. (1983). *Stages of reading development.* McGraw Hill.

Cipielewski, J., & Stanovich, K. E. (1992). Predicting growth in reading ability form children's exposure to print. *Journal of Experimental Child Psychology, 54*(1), 74–89.

Clark, A., & Fleming, J. (2019). "They Almost Become the Teacher": Pre-K to third grade teachers' experiences reading and discussing culturally relevant texts with their students. *Reading Horizons: A Journal of Literacy and Language Arts, 58*(3).

Clay, M. (1993). *An observation survey of early literacy achievement.* Heinemann.

Cloud, N., Genesee, F., & Hamayan, E. (2009). *Literacy instruction for English language learners: A teacher's guide to research-based practices.* Heinemann.

Collett, J., & Dubetz, N. (2021). Instruction to engage multilingual learners with grade-level content. *The Reading Teacher, 75*(5), 593–602.

Collins, A., Hawkins, J., & Carver, S. M. (1991). *A cognitive apprenticeship for disadvantaged students* (final report). Teaching Advanced Skills to Educationally Disadvantaged Students (pp. 173–194). United States Department of Education (USDE).

Coxhead, A. (2000). AWL most frequent words in sublists. https://www.wgtn.ac.nz/lals/resources/academicwordlist/most-frequent

Cummins, J. (1979). Linguistic interdependence and the educational development of bilingual children. *Review of Educational Research, 49*(2), 222–251.

Cummins, J. (1981). Four misconceptions about language proficiency in bilingual education. *NABE: The Journal for the National Association for Bilingual Education, 5*(3), 17–31.

Cummins, J. (1984). Bilingualism and special education: Issues in assessment and pedagogy. *Learning Disability Quarterly, 6*(4), 373–386.

Cummins, J. (1996). *Negotiating identities: Education for empowerment in a diverse society.* California Association for Bilingual Education.

Cummins, J. (2000). *Language, power, and pedagogy: Bilingual children in the crossfire.* Multilingual Matters.

Cummins, J. (2010). Translanguaging: A critical analysis of theoretical claims. In P. Juvonen & M. Källkvist (Eds.), *Pedagogical translanguaging: Theoretical, methodological and empirical perspectives.* Multilingual Matters.

Cummins, J. (2011). Literacy engagement: Fueling academic growth for English learners. *The Reading Teacher, 65*(2), 142–146.

Cunningham, A. E., & Stanovich, K. E. (1997). Early reading acquisition and its relation to reading experience and ability 10 years later. *Developmental Psychology, 33*(6), 934–945.

Dazzeo, R., & Rao, K. (2020). Digital Frayer model: Supporting vocabulary acquisition with technology and UDL. *Teaching Exceptional Children, 53*(1), 34–42.

Degener, S., & Berne, J. (2016). Complex questions promote complex thinking. *The Reading Teacher, 70*(5), 595–599.

De Jong, E. J., & Harper, C. A. (2005). Preparing mainstream teachers for English-language learners: Is being a good teacher good enough? *Teacher Education Quarterly, 32*(2), 101–124.

Duff, F. J., Reen, G., Plunket, K., & Nation, K. (2015). Do infant vocabulary skills predict school-age language and literacy outcomes? *Journal of child psychology, 56*(8), 848–856.

Duke, N. K., & Block, M. K. (2012). Improving reading in the primary grades. *Future of Children, 22*(2), 55–72.

Duke, N., Pearson, D., Strachan, S., & Billman, A. (2011). Essential elements of fostering and teaching reading comprehension. In S. J. Samuels & A. E. Farstrup (Eds.), *What research has to say about reading instruction* (pp. 51–93). International Reading Association.

Echevarria, J., & Graves, A. (2002). *Sheltered content instruction: Teaching English-language learners with diverse abilities* (2nd ed.). Allyn & Bacon.

Echevarria, J., & Vogt, M. E. (2010). Using the SIOP model to improve literacy for English learners. *New England Reading Association Journal, 46*(1), 8–15, 109, 111.

Edelman, E. R., Amirazizi, S. A., Feinberg, D. K, Quirk, M., Scheller, J., Pagán, C. R., & Persoon, J. (2022). A comparison of integrated and designated ELD models on second and third graders' oral English language proficiency. *TESOL Journal, 13*(3).

Ehri, L. C. (2005). Learning to read words: Theory, findings, and issues. *Scientific Studies of Reading, 9*, 167–188.

Ehri, L. C. (2011). Teaching phonemic awareness and phonics in the language arts classroom. In D. Lapp & D. Fisher (Eds.), *Handbook of research on teaching the English language arts* (3rd ed.). Routledge.

Ehri, L. C., & McCormick, S. (1998). Phases of word learning: Implications for instruction with delayed and disabled readers. *Reading & Writing Quarterly, 14*(2), 135–163.

Elley, W. B. (1991). Acquiring literacy in a second language: The effect of book-based programs. *Language learning, 41*(3), 375–411.

Ellis, R., & Shintani, N. (2013). *Exploring language pedagogy through second language acquisition research.* Routledge.

Fareed, M., Ashraf, A., & Bilal, M. (2016). ESL learners' writing skills: Problems, factors and suggestions. *Journal of Education and Social Sciences, 4*, 81–92.

Feng, Y., & Webb. S. (2020). Learning vocabulary through reading, listening, and viewing. *Studies in Second Language Acquisition, 42*(3), 499–523.

Fisher, D., Frey, N., & Akhavan, N. (2019). *This is balanced literacy.* Corwin.

Foorman, B. R., & Connor, C. (2011). Primary reading. In M. Kamil, P. D. Pearson, & E. Moje (Eds.), *Handbook on reading research* (Vol. 4, pp. 136–156).

Francis, E. M. (2017, May 9). What is Webb's depth of knowledge? *ASCD* blog. https://www.ascd.org/blogs/what-exactly-is-depth-of-knowledge-hint-its-not-a-wheel

Freeman, D., & Freeman, Y. (2014). *Essential linguistics: What teachers need to know to* teach ESL, reading, spelling and grammar (2nd ed.). Heinemann.

Freyd, P., & Baron, J. (1982). Individual differences in acquisition of derivational morphology. *Journal of Verbal Learning and Verbal Behavior, 21*(3), 282–295.

Gamez, P. B. (2009). *Academic oral language development in Spanish-speaking English language learners: The effect of teacher talk.* The University of Chicago; ProQuest Dissertations Publishing.

Gamez, P. B. (2015). Classroom-based English exposure and English language learners' expressive language skills. *Early Childhood Research Quarterly, 31,* 135–146.

Gándara, P. (2018). The economic value of bilingualism in the United States. *Bilingual Research Journal, 41*(4), 334–343.

García, S. B., & Malkin, D. H. (1993). Toward defining program and services for culturally and linguistically diverse learners in special education. *Teaching Exceptional Children, 26*(1), 52–58.

Genesee, F. (1999). *Program alternatives for linguistically diverse students.* UC Berkeley: Center for Research on Education, Diversity and Excellence. https://escholarship.org/uc/item/95t956xz

Genesee, F., Lindholm-Leary, K., Saunders, W., & Christian, D. (2005). English language learners in U.S. schools: An overview of research findings. *Journal of Education for Students Placed at Risk, 10*(4), 363–385.

Genesee, F., & Riches, C. (2006). Literacy: Instructional issues. In F. Genesee, K. Lindholm-Leary, W. Saunder, & D. Christian (Eds.), *Educating English language learners* (pp. 363–384). Cambridge.

Gentry, J. R. (1982). Developmental aspects of learning to spell. *Intervention in School and Clinic, 20*(1), 11–19.

Gibbons, P. (2009). *English learners, academic literacy and thinking.* Heinemann.

Gibbons, P. (2015). *Scaffolding language, scaffolding learning: Teaching English language learners in the mainstream classroom.* Heineman.

Gillingham, A., & Stillman, B.W. (1997). *The Gillingham manual: Remedial training for children with specific disability in reading, spelling, and penmanship* (8th ed.). Educators Publishing Service.

Goldenburg, C. (2010). Improving achievement for English learners: Conclusions from recent reviews and emerging research. In G. Li & P. A. Edwards (Eds.), *Best practices in ELL instruction* (pp. 15–43). Guilford Publications.

Gomez, L., Freeman, D., & Freeman, Y. (2010). Dual language education: A promising 50–50 model. *Bilingual Research Journal, 29*(1), 145–164.

Gonzalez, J. (2007). The power of songs: Why and how does music improve language learning? *Computer Science.*

Gooch, K., & Lambirth, A. (2008). *Understanding phonics and the teaching of reading.* McGraw-Hill Education.

Goswami, U., & Mead, F. (1992). Onset and rime awareness and analogies in reading. *Reading Research Quarterly, 27,* 152–162.

Gottlieb, M. (2006). *Assessing English language learners.* Corwin.

Gottlieb, M. (2016). *Assessing English language learners: Bridges to educational equity: connecting academic language proficiency to student achievement* (2nd ed.). Corwin.

Gough, P. B., & Tunmer, W. E. (1986). Decoding, reading, and reading disability. *Remedial and Special Education, 7*(1), 6–10.

Grabe, W., & Zhang, C. (2013). Reading and writing together: A critical component of English for academic purposes teaching and learning. *TESOL Journal, 41*(1), 9–24.

Granados, A., López-Jiménez, M. D., & Lorenzo, F. (2022). A longitudinal study of L2 historical writing: Lexical richness and writing proficiency in content and language integrated learning. *Iberica 43,* 129–143.

Graves, M. F., & Watts-Taffe, S. (2008). For the love of words: Fostering word consciousness in young readers. *The Reading Teacher, 62*(3), 185–193.

Gutherie, J. T., & Barber, A. T. (2019). Best practices for motivating students to read. In L. M. Morrow & L. B. Grambrell (Eds.), *Best practice in literacy instruction* (pp. 52–72). Guilford Press.

Gutierrez, K. D., Zepeda, M., & Castro, D. C. (2010). Advancing early literacy learning for all children: Implications of the NELP report for dual-language learners. *Educational Researcher, 39*(4), 334–339.

Haigh, C. A., Savage, R., Erdos, C., & Genesee, F. (2011). The role of phoneme and onset-rime awareness in second language reading acquisition. *Journal of Research in Reading, 34*(1), 94–11.

Harvey, S., & Goudvis, A. (2013). Comprehension at the core. *The Reading Teacher, 66*(6), 432–439.

Hattie, J. (2008). *Visible learning: A synthesis of over 800 meta-analyses relating to achievement.* Routledge.

Haynes, J. (2007). *Getting started with English learners: How educators can meet the challenge.* ASCD.

Heibeck, T. H., & Markman, E. M. (1987). Word learning in children: An examination of fast mapping. *Child Development, 58*(4), 1021–1034.

Helman, L. (2016a). Effective instructional practices for emergent bilinguals. In L. Helman (Ed.), *Literacy development with English learners: Research-based instruction in grades K–6,* (2nd ed., pp. 309–328). Guilford Press.

Helman. L. (2016b). Emergent literacy: Planting the seeds for accomplished reading and writing. In L. Helman (Ed.), *Literacy Development With English Learners: Research-based instruction in grades K–6* (2nd ed., pp. 141–163). Guilford Press.

Helman, L., & Bear, D. R. (2007). Does an established model of orthographic development hold true for English learners? In D. W. Rowe, R. Jimenez, D. L. Compton, D. K. Dickinson, Y. Kim, K. M. Leander, & V. J. Risko (Eds.), *56th yearbook for the National Reading Conference* (pp. 266–280). National Reading Conference.

Helman, L., Ittner, A. C., & McMaster, K. L. (2019). *Assessing language and literacy with bilingual students: Practices to support English learners.* Guilford Press.

Henry, M. K. (1993). Morphological structure: Latin and Greek roots and affixes as upper grade code strategies. *Reading and Writing, 5*(2), 227–241.

Hiebert, E. (2019). *Teaching words and how they work: Small changes for big vocabulary results.* Teachers College Press.

Himmele, P., & Himmele, W. (2009). *The language-rich classroom.* ASCD.

Hoff, E. (2013). *Language development.* Cengage.

Honigsfeld, A., & Dove, M. G. (2013). *Collaborating for English learners: A foundational guide to integrated practices* (2nd ed.). Corwin.

Horst, M., White, J., & Bell, P. (2010). First and second language knowledge in the language classroom. *International Journal of Bilingualism, 14*(3), 331–349.

Hoyt, L. (2016). *Interactive read-alouds, grades 2–3: Linking standards, fluency, and comprehension.* Heinemann.

Invernizzi, M., & Hayes, L. (2004). Theory and research into practice: Developmental-spelling research: A systematic imperative. *Reaching Research Quarterly, 39*(2), 216–228.

Keck, C. (2006). The use of paraphrase in summary writing: A comparison of L1 and L2 writers. *Journal of Second Language Writing, 15*(4), 261–278.

Kersten, S. (2010). *The mental lexicon and vocabulary learning: Implications for the foreign language classroom.* Books on Demand.

Kessler, B., & Treiman, R. (2015). Writing systems: Their properties and implications for reading. In A. Pollatsek & R. Treiman (Eds.), *The Oxford handbook of reading* (pp. 10–25). Oxford University Press.

Kieffer, M. J. (2012). Early oral language and later reading development in Spanish-speaking English language learners: Evidence from a nine-year longitudinal study. *Journal of Applied Developmental Psychology, 33,* 146–157.

Kieffer, M. J., & Lesaux, N. K. (2007). Breaking down words to build meaning: Morphology, vocabulary, and reading comprehension in the urban classroom:

When it comes to teaching vocabulary, a little knowledge (of root words, prefixes, and suffixes) goes a long way. *The Reading Teacher, 61*(2), 134–144.

Kieffer, M. J., & Lesaux, N. K. (2012). Knowledge of words, knowledge about words: Dimensions of vocabulary in first and second language learners in sixth grade. *Reading and Writing: An Interdisciplinary Journal, 25*, 347–373.

Kilpatrick, D. A. (2015). *Essentials of assessing and overcoming reading disabilities.* Wiley.

Kim, A., Vaughn, S., Wanzek J., & Wei, S. (2004). Graphic organizers and their effects on the reading comprehension of students with LD: A synthesis of research. *Journal of Learning Disabilities, 37*, 105–118. doi:10.1177/00222194040370020201

Kindervater, T. M. (2012). *A case study of teaching phonemic awareness to parents and children: Scaffolded preschool tutoring with kinesthetic motions for phonemes* [Dissertation publication number 3510733]. Kent State University, ProQuest Dissertations Publishing.

Kohnert, K., & Pham, G. (2010). The process of acquiring first and second languages. In M. Shatz & L. Wilkinson (Eds.), *Preparing to educate English language learners* (pp. 48–66). Guilford.

Kong, A., & Fitch, E. (2002). Using book club to engage culturally and linguistically diverse learners in reading, writing, and talking about books. *The Reading Teacher, 56*(4), 352–362.

Koskinen, P. S., Gambrell, L. B., Kapinus, B. A., & Heathington, B. S. (1988). Retelling: A strategy for enhancing students' reading comprehension. *The Reading Teacher, 41*(9), 892–896. https://www.jstor.org/stable/20199962

Krashen, S. D. (1982). *Principles and practices in second language acquisition.* Pergamon Press.

Krashen, S. D. (1988). *Second language acquisition and second language learning.* Prentice Hall.

Krashen, S., & Mason, B. (2017). Sustained silent reading in foreign language education: An update. *Turkish Online Journal of English Language Teaching 2*(2), 70–73.

Kruk, R. S., & Bergman, K. (2013). The reciprocal relations between morphological processes and reading. *Journal of Experimental Child Psychology, 114*, 10–34.

James, I., & Carter, T. S. (2007). Questioning and informational texts: Scaffolding students' comprehension of content areas. *Forum on Public Policy, 2007*(3), 1–13.

January, S. A., Lovelace, M.A., Foster, T. E., & Ardoin, S. P (2017). A comparison of two flashcard interventions for teaching sight words to early readers. *Journal of Behavioral Education 26*, 151–168.

Johnston, S. S., Tulbert, B. L., Sebastian, J. P., Devries, K., & Gompert, A. (2000). Vocabulary development: A collaborative effort for teaching content vocabulary. *Intervention in School and Clinic, 35*(5), 311–313.

Joseph, L. M., & Ross, K. M. (2017). Teaching middle school students with learning disabilities to comprehend text using self-questioning. *Intervention School Climate, 53*, 276–282.

LaBerge, D. L., & Samuels, S. J. (1974). Toward a theory of automatic information processing in reading. *Cognitive Psychology, 6*(2), 293–323.

Laufer, B. (2010). Form-focused instruction in second language vocabulary learning. In R. Chacón-Beltrán, C. Abello-Contesse, & M. del Mar Torreblanca-López (Eds.), *Insights into non-native vocabulary teaching and learning* (pp. 15–27). Channel View Publications.

Laufer, B., & Hulstjin, J. H. (2001). Incidental vocabulary acquisition in a secondary language: The construct of task-induced involvement. *Applied Linguistics, 22*(1), 1–26.

Lightbown, P. M., & Spada, N. (1990). Focus-on-form and corrective feedback in communicative language teaching: Effects on second language learning. *Studies in Second Language Acquisition, 12*, 429–448.

Lucero, A. (2018). The development of bilingual narrative retelling among Spanish-English dual language learners over two years. *Language, Speech and Hearing Services in Schools, 49*(3), 607–621.

Manyak, P. C., Baumann, J. F., & Manyak, A. M. (2018). Morphological analysis instruction in the elementary grades: Which morphemes to teach and how to teach them. *The Reading Teacher, 72*(3), 289–300.

Marzano, R. J., Pickering, D., & Pollock, J. E. (2001). *Classroom instruction that works: Research-based strategies for increasing student achievement.* ASCD.

Mathes, P. G., Denton, C. A., Fletcher, J. M., Anthony, J. L., Francis, D. J., & Schatschneider, C. (2007). An evaluation of two reading interventions derived from diverse models. *Reading Research Quarterly, 40,* 148–183.

McIntyre, S., & Hulan, N. (2013). Research-based, culturally responsive reading practice in elementary classrooms: A yearlong study. *Literacy Research and Instruction, 52*(1), 28–51.

McIntyre, E., Kyle, D., Cheng-Teng, C., Muñoz, M., & Beldon, S. (2010). Teacher learning and ELL reading achievement in sheltered instruction classrooms: Linking professional development to student development, *Literacy Research and Instruction, 49*(4), 334–351.

McKay, S. L. (2006). *Researching second language classrooms.* Routledge.

Melby-Lervåg, M., & Lervåg, A. (2014). Reading comprehension and its underlying components in second-language learners: A meta-analysis of studies comparing first- and second-language learners. *Psychology Bulletin, 140*(2), 409–433.

Miramontes, O. B., Nadeau, A., & Commins, N. L. (1997). *Restructuring schools for linguistic diversity: Linking decision making to effective programs.* Teachers College Press.

Mitchell, C. (2020). How will schools teach English-language learners this fall: *Education Week.* https://www.edweek.org/teaching-learning/how-will-schools-teach-english-language-learners-this-fall/2020/09

Molden, K. (2007). Critical literacy, the right answer for the reading classroom: Strategies to move beyond comprehension for reading improvement. *Reading Improvement, 44*(1), 50–56.

Montelongo, J. A., Hernández, A. C., Herter, R. J., & Cuello, J. (2011). Using cognates to scaffold context clue strategies for Latino ELs. *The Reading Teacher, 64*(6), 429–434.

Montero, M. K., & Kuhn, M. R. (2016). English learners and fluency development: More than speed and accuracy. In L. Helman (Ed.), *Literacy development with English learners: Research-based instruction in grades K–6* (2nd ed., pp. 182–205). Guilford Press.

Moschkovich, J. (1999). Supporting the participation of English language learners in mathematical discussions. *For the Learning of Mathematics, 19*(1), 11–19.

Moss, B. (2005). Making a case and a place for effective content area literacy instruction in the elementary grades. *The Reading Teacher, 59*(1), 46–55.

Moschkovich, J. (1999). Supporting the participation of English language learners in mathematical discussions. *For the Learning of Mathematics, 19*(1), 11–19.

Mountain, L. (2015). Recurrent prefixes, roots, and suffixes: A morphemic approach to disciplinary literacy. *Journal of Adolescent & Adult Literacy, 58*(7), 561–567.

Nagy, W. E. (1988). *Teaching vocabulary to improve reading comprehension.* National Council of Teachers of English.

Nagy, W. E., & Anderson, R. C. (1984). How many words are there in printed school English? *Reading Research Quarterly, 19*(3), 304–330.

Nagy, W., Berninger, V. W., & Abbot, R. D. (2006). Contributions of morphology beyond phonology to literacy outcomes of upper elementary and middle-school students. *Journal of Educational Psychology, 98*(1), 134–147.

Nation, I. S. P. (2001). *Learning vocabulary in another language.* Cambridge University Press.

National Early Literacy Panel. (NELP). (2008). Developing early literacy: A scientific synthesis of early literacy development and implications for intervention.

National Governors Association Center for Best Practices, Council of Chief State School Officers. (2010). *Common core state standards (English language arts)*. National Governors Association Center for Best Practices, Council of Chief State School Officers.

Ness, M. K. (2016). Reading comprehension strategies in secondary content area classrooms: Teacher use of and attitudes towards reading comprehension instruction. *Reading Horizons: A Journal of Literacy and Language Arts, 49*(2). https://scholarworks.wmich.edu/reading_horizons/vol49/iss2/5

Nirchi, S. (2014). Assessing learners' reading literacy through new approaches: The construction and integration model. *International Journal of Digital Literacy and Digital Competence, 5*(2).

NSW. (2022). NSW Government website. https://education.nsw.gov.au/teaching-and-learning/curriculum/literacy-and-numeracy/teaching-and-learning-resources/literacy/effective-reading-in-the-early-years-of-school/phonics

Olson, C. B., Matuchniak, T., Chung, H. Q., Stumpf, R., & Farkas, G. (2017). Reducing achievement gaps in academic writing for Latinos and English learners in grades 7–12. *Journal of Educational Psychology, 109*(1), 1–21.

Olson, C. B., Scarcella, R., & Matuchniak, T. (2015). English learners, writing, and the common core. *Elementary School Journal, 115*(4), 570–592. https://doi.org/10.1086/681235

Ortiz, A. A., & Franquiz, M. E. (2019). Co-editors introduction: Challenges to the success of English learners in the context of language instruction educational programs. *Bilingual Research Journal, 42*(1), 1–5.

Palmer, C. (1994). *Developing cultural literacy through the writing process: Empowering all learners*. Allyn & Bacon.

Park, B. J., Foley, A., & Bates, R. B. (2021). *How NAEP's oral reading fluency study informs literacy instruction*. https://www.air.org/resource/qa/how-naeps-oral-reading-fluency-study-informs-literacy-instruction

Pearson, P. D., & Gallagher, M. C. (1983). The instruction of reading comprehension. *Contemporary Educational Psychology, 8*(3), 317–344.

Peregoy, S. F., & Boyle, O. F. (1997). *Reading, writing and learning in ESL: A resource book for K–12 teachers* (3rd ed.). Pearson.

Peregoy, S. F., & Boyle, O. F. (2000). English learners reading English: What we know, what we need to know. *Theory Into Practice, 39*(4), 237–247.

Peregoy, S. F., & Boyle, O. F. (2016). *Reading, writing and learning in ESL: A resource book for K–12 teachers* (7th ed.). Pearson.

Pérez, B. (2004). *Sociocultural context of language and literacy* (2nd ed.). Lawrence Erlbaum.

Perry, N. E., Turner, J. C., & Meyer, D. K. (2006). Classrooms as contexts for motivating learning. In P. A. Alexander & P. H. Winnie (Eds.), *Handbook of educational psychology* (pp. 327–348). Routledge.

Phantharkphong, P., & Pothitha, S. (2014). Development of English reading comprehension by using concept maps. *Procedia Social and Behavioral Sciences, 116*, 497–501.

Pitts, M. M. (1983). Comprehension monitoring: Definition and practice. *Journal of Reading, 26*, 516–523.

Pressley, M. (2006). *Reading instruction that works: The case for balanced teaching* (3rd ed.). Guilford Press.

Pressley, M. (2015). *Reading instruction that works: The case for balanced teaching*. Guilford Press.

Pressley, M., Brown, R., El-Dinary, P. B., & Allferbach, P. (1995). The comprehension instruction that students need: Instruction fostering constructively responsive reading. *Learning Disabilities Research & Practice, 10*(4), 215–224.

Pressley, M., & Wharton-McDonald, R. (1997). Skilled comprehension and its development through instruction. *School Psychology Review, 26*(3), 448–466.

Ramsey, J. (2019). *Teaching academic vocabulary to increase comprehension in content areas for ELLs from grades 3–5*. ProQuest Dissertations & Theses Global; The Humanities and Social Sciences Collection.

Raphael, T. (1982). *Improving question-answering performance through instruction* (Reading Education Report No. 32). University of Illinois at Urbana-Champaign: Center for the Study of Reading.

Raphael, T. E., & Au, K. H. (2005). QAR: Enhancing comprehension and test taking across grades and content areas. *The Reading Teacher, 59*(3), 206–221.

Rapp, D. N., van den Broek, P., McMaster, K. L., Kendeou, P., & Espin, C. A. (2007). *Higher-order comprehension processes in struggling readers: A perspective for research and intervention.*

Rasinski, T. V. (2010). *The fluent reader: Oral and silent reading strategies for building word recognition, fluency, and comprehension* (2nd ed.). Scholastic.

Rasinski, T., Homan, S., & Biggs, M. (2008). Teaching reading fluency to struggling readers: Method, materials, and evidence. *Reading and Writing Quarterly, 25*(2–3).

Rasinski, T. V., Padak, N., Newton, J., & Newton, E. (2011). The Latin-Greek connection: Building vocabulary through morphological study. *The Reading Teacher, 65*(2), 133–142.

Rasinski, T. V., Reutzel, D. R., Chard, D., & Linan-Thompson, S. (2011). Reading fluency. In M. L. Kamil, P. D. Pearson, E. B. Moje, & P. P. Afflerbach (Eds.), *Handbook of reading research* (Vol. IV, pp. 286–319). Routledge.

Rasinski, T., & Young, C. (2014). Assisted reading—A bridge from fluency to comprehension. *New England Reading Association Journal, 50*(1), 1–4.

Robb, L. (2022). *Increase reading volume: Practical strategies that boost students' achievement and passion for reading*. National Council of Teachers of English.

Romero-Little, M. E. (2010). How should young indigenous children be prepared for learning?: A vision of early childhood education for indigenous children. *Journal of American Indian Education, 49*(1–2), 7–27.

Sailors, M., & Price, L. R. (2015). Support for the improvement of practices through intensive coaching (SIPIC): A model of coaching for improving reading instruction and reading achievement. *Teaching and Teacher Education, 45.*

Samuels, J. (1974). The method of repeated readings. *The Reading Teacher, 50*(5), 376–381.

Scarborough, H. S. (2001). Connecting early language and literacy to later reading (dis)abilities: Evidence, theory, and practice. In S. B. Neuman & D. K. Dickinson (Eds.), *Handbook of early literacy research* (Vol. 1, pp. 97–110). Guilford.

Scarcella, R. (2003). *Academic English: A conceptual framework* (Technical Report 2003-1). University of California Linguistic Minority Research Institute.

Schumaker, J. B., Denton, P. H., & Deshler, D. D. (1984). *The paraphrasing strategy*. University of Kansas Press.

SEAL. (2021). SEAL website. https://seal.org/

Serafini, F. (2014). Exploring wordless picture books. *The Reading Teacher, 68*(1), 24–26. https://doi.org/10.1002/trtr.1294

Shanahan, T. (2020). *How much phonics should I teach?* Shanahanonliteracy.com. https://www.shanahanonliteracy.com/blog/how-much-phonics-should-i-teach#sthash.bfq7D5lC.dpbs

Shanahan, T., & Beck, I. L. (2006). Effective literacy teaching for English-language learners. In D. August & T. Shanahan (Eds.), *Developing literacy in second-language learners: Report of the National Literacy Panel on Language-Minority Children and Youth* (pp. 415–488). Erlbaum.

Shi, L. (2004). Textual borrowing in second-language writing. *Written Communication, 21*(2), 171–200. https://doi.org/10.1177/0741088303262846

Sibold, C. (2011). Building English language learners' academic vocabulary: Strategies & tips. *Multicultural Education, 18*(2), 24–28.

Snider, V. A. (1995). A primer on phonemic awareness: What it is, why it's important, and how to teach it. *School Psychology Review, 24*(3).

Snow, C. E. (2017). Early literacy development and instruction: An overview. In N. Kucirkova, C. E. Snow, V. Grøver, & C. McBride-Chang (Eds.), *The Routledge international handbook of early literacy education: A contemporary guide to literacy teaching and interventions in a global context* (pp. 5–13). Routledge.

Snow, C. E., Griffin, P., & Burns, M. S. (Eds.). (2005). *Knowledge to support the teaching of reading.* Jossey-Bass.

Snow, C. E., & Kim, Y.-S. (2007). Large problem spaces: The challenge of vocabulary for English language learners. In R. K. Wagner, A. E. Muse, & K. R. Tannenbaum (Eds.), *Vocabulary acquisition: Implications for reading comprehension* (pp. 123–139). Guilford Press.

Spear-Swerling, L., & Chessman, E. (2015). Teachers' knowledge base for implementing response-to-intervention models in reading. *Reading and Writing 25*(7), 1691–1723.

Spycher, P. (2007). Academic writing of adolescent English learners: Learning to use "although." *Journal of Second Language Writing, 16*(4), 238–254.

Stahl, S. A. (2004). What do we know about fluency? Findings of the national reading panel. In P. McCardle & V. Chhabra (Eds.), *The voice of evidence in reading research* (pp. 187–211). Paul H. Brookes Publishing.

Steele, J., Slater, R., Zamarro, G., Miller, T., Li, J., Burkhauser, S., & Bacon, M. (2017). Effects of dual-language immersion programs on student achievement: Evidence from lottery data. *American Educational Research Journal, 54*, 282–306.

Stoutz, S. (2011). *Retelling using different methods* [Dissertation]. Education Masters. Paper 199. https://fisherpub.sjfc.edu/education_ETD_masters/199

Swiegart, W. (1991). Classroom talk, knowledge development, and writing. *Research in the Teaching of English, 25*(4), 469–496.

Templeton, S. (2020). Stages, phases, repertoires, and waves: Learning to spell and read words. *The Reading Teacher, 74*(3), 315–323.

Templeton, S., & Bear, D. (2017). Word study, research to practice: Spelling, phonics, meaning. In D. Lapp & D. Fisher (Eds.), *Handbook of research on teaching the language arts* (4th ed.). Guilford.

Tharp, R. G. (1997). *From at-risk to excellence: Research, theory, and principles for practice* (Research Report No. 1). Center for Applied Linguistics and Center for Research on Education, Diversity, and Excellence.

Tolman, C. (2005). Working smarter, not harder: What teachers of reading need to know and be able to teach. *Perspectives, 31*, 16–24.

Tong, F., Lara-Alecio, R., Irby, B., Mathes, P., & Oi-man, K. (2008). Accelerating early academic oral English development in transitional bilingual and structured English immersion programs. *American Educational Research Journal, 45*(4), 1011–1044.

Treiman, R. (2017). Learning to spell: Phonology and beyond. *Cognitive Neuropsychology, 34*(3–4), 83–93.

Treiman, R., & Kessler, B. (2014). *How children learn to write words.* Oxford University Press.

Tudor, I., & Hafiz, F. (1989). Extensive reading as a means of input to L2 learning. *Journal of Research in Reading, 12*(2), 164–178. https://doi.org/10.1111/j.1467-9817.1989.tb00164.x

Tyner, B. *Small-group reading instruction: A differentiated teaching model for beginning and struggling readers* (2nd ed.). International Reading Association.

Ukrainetz, T. A., Cooney, M. H., Dyer, S. K., Kysar, A. J., & Harris, T. J. (2000). An investigation into teaching phonemic awareness through shared reading and writing. *Early Childhood Research Quarterly, 15*(3), 331–355.

U.S. Census Bureau. (2021). *Quick facts statistics for all states and counties.* Retrieved from https://www.census.gov/quickfacts/fact/table/US/PST045218

Varnhagen, C. K., Mccallum, M., & Burstow, M. (1997). Is children's spelling naturally stage-like? *Reading and Writing: An Interdisciplinary Journal, 9,* 451–481.

Vaughn, S., Wanzek, J., Woodruff, A. L., & Linan-Thompson, S. (2007). Prevention and early identification of students with reading disabilities. In D. Haager, J. Klinger, & S. Vaughn (Eds.), *Evidence-based reading practices for response to intervention* (pp. 11–28). Paul H. Brookes Publishing.

Walpole, S., & McKenna, M. C. (2007). *Differentiated reading instruction: Strategies for the primary grades.* Guilford Publications.

Wang, J. H.-Y., & Guthrie, J. T. (2004). Modeling the effects of intrinsic motivation, extrinsic motivation, amount of reading, and past reading achievement on text comprehension between U.S. and Chinese students. *Reading Research Quarterly, 39*(2), 162–186.

Westwood, P. S. (2001). *Reading and learning difficulties: Approaches to teaching and assessment* (2nd ed.). Australian Council for Education Research.

Wharton-McDonald, R. (2014). Expert literacy teaching in the primary grades. In M. Pressley & R. L. Allington, *Reading instruction that works: The case for balanced teaching* (4th ed.). Guilford Press.

WIDA. (2019). *ELD standards framework.* https://wida.wisc.edu/teach/standards/eld

Wilkinson, I. A. G., & Son, E. H. (2011). A dialogic turn research on learning and teaching to comprehend. In M. L. Kamil, P. D. Pearson, E. B. Moje, & P. P. Afflerbac (Eds.), *Handbook of reading research* (Vol. IV, pp. 359–387). Routledge.

Wood, N. (1999). *Silly Sally.* Clarion.

Wright, W. E. (2019). *Foundations for teaching English language learners: Research, theory, policy, and practice.* Caslon.

Young, K. (2007). Developmental stage theory of spelling: Analysis of consistency across four spelling-related activities. *Australian Journal of Language and Literacy, 11*(3).

Young, T. A., & Hadaway, N. L. (2006). *Supporting the literacy development of English learners.* International Reading Association.

Index